ORGANI[...] HAPPINESS

THE HAPPINESS SWEET SPOT
AND YOUR MOTIVATIONAL
LANDSCAPE

LARS KURE JUUL

Clearsight Publishing
COPENHAGEN

Clearsight Publishing
Nybrogade 26
Copenhagen
www.TheHappinessSweetSpot.com
www.MotivationalLandscape.com

Ordering Information:
Quantity sales. Special discounts are available on quantity purchases by corporations, associations, and others. For details, contact the publisher.

Organizational Happiness / Lars Kure Juul. — 1st ed.
ISBN 978-87-971055-0-4

Contents

To my Angel!
You make me happy!

ABOUT THIS BOOK

This book is dedicated to leaders and organizational professionals. They are in the position to facilitate and catalyze organizational and business development and can spark action and change behavior. If you want to strengthen and improve the bottom line of your organization, you should move from strategy to action on organizational happiness and employee engagement.

This book is meant to be short, sweet, and to the point. I want to inspire you to take action. And I will do my best to give you a way to get on the fast track from strategy to action based on research, cases, and my experience from the last twenty years as an executive and trusted advisor in different industries and different settings in many parts of the world.

This book will inspire you to take organizational happiness and employee engagement seriously. I will present the pillars for organizational happiness, explain why it is a competitive advantage, and help you build a business case, and I will give you a simple framework to work strategically with organizational happiness and employee engagement as an engine for high performance and sustainable success.

I believe that there is a lot of unused and unlocked potential in organizations and that organizational happiness and employee engagement is the key that can unlock that potential in an effective and sustainable way.

Organizations with happy, engaged employees simply create better results.

For happy employees in a society where people struggle with mental health, are stressed, and long for motivation, purpose, and meaning, this message will make sense, and they will be able to help others overcome these challenges. That is how I see myself making a little contribution to the universe—when I inspire action.

This book is structured so you can make it yours. Define your own Organizational Happiness Sweet Spot and go from strategy to action. Fast.

First, I will introduce the concept of organizational happiness and the science of happiness. Then I will apply it to business and give you the recipe for success, just to get you ignited. Then we dive into the "how" and "why" of each of the three pillars of organizational happiness. And at the end I will give you a way to measure, monitor, and follow up on your organizational happiness strategy.

FOREWORD

Organizations are not problems to be solved, but mysteries to be embraced.

—David Cooperrider

I first met Lars nearly a decade ago in Central America. He had traveled from his home in Copenhagen to the University for Peace, headquartered in Costa Rica, for a workshop titled "Positive Leadership." His background as a lawyer, CEO, international HR professional, C-level consultant, and author combined with his keen interest in working with organizations with a purpose resonated deeply with the work we do at the United Nations–mandated University for Peace via its Centre for Executive Education.

More than three thousand participants from all continents have gone through our on-site, online, and customized programs since 2006, when our Centre for Executive Education was launched. But there is one question that is core to all of our workshops. In its simplest form, it is "What makes you happy?" Yes, all of us want to be happy. The United Nations recently recognized the importance of giving more visibility to this universal human desire, and March 20, 2012, was declared the first United Nations International Day of Happiness. The UN's Sustainable Development Goals also explicitly refer to the importance of aiming to "ensure healthy lives and promote well-being for all at all ages" (Goal 3). In organizations, anyone who is not able to renew his or her energy and learn to appreciate the bumpy journey of professional life in the twenty-first century will at best be much less effective than their potential and at worst burn out. The effect is both personal and professional.

Lars's book is timely, because there is a disconnect between the science of happiness and its implementation in organizations. Fascinating new research is emerging from the field of positive psychology that helps unpack complex questions surrounding the conditions for happiness. A primary framework comes from Dr. Martin Seligman, widely viewed as the father of positive psychology. He asserts that happiness (he prefers the term *flourishing*) is about five elements, captured by the acronym PERMA:

- experiencing ***Positive*** emotions (**P**)
- being ***Engaged*** with what you do (**E**)
- building strong ***Relationships*** (**R**)
- feeling that your life has ***Meaning*** beyond yourself (**M**)
- having a sense of personal ***Achievement*** (**A**)

In *Organizational Happiness*, Lars takes PERMA to the next level, discussing how it can be operationalized across organizations. To be relevant in the twenty-first century, he says, organizations must have clarity around their purpose. People within organizations need to identify their strengths and work in those areas, which will lead to deep engagement. Building an organizational culture that promotes positive relationships and cultivates compassion is critical. In this way, achievement, or bottom-line results, becomes an outcome of organizational happiness, rather than the sole objective—a case in which the "means justify the end" rather than the other way around.

The world is changing at an increasingly fast pace, affecting how we communicate, how we bank, how we vacation, and certainly how we make purchasing decisions. The effect on the business world is profound. But despite technological advances and how they influence human behavior, we can confidently say that the question "What makes you happy?" is not going to become obsolete and will in fact become increasingly relevant.

Organizational Happiness offers insights into what leaders of organizations need to do to be able to attract, motivate, and retain people who are looking at work as much more than a paycheck. The trend toward a younger workforce—made up of millennials—looking for more purpose and autonomy in their work is one that every mature organization is going to need to address. In the United States, millennials had become the largest generation as of 2015, and that change happened earlier in many countries. As a Gen Xer who works mainly with millennials, I once underestimated how challenging it is to create a happy workplace. Today, I think that building a workplace environment that allows millennials to flourish is not just a "nice to have" but is critical to having a flourishing organization.

Over the years, Lars has become a friend, a collaborator, and a trusted advisor. His work embeds the University for Peace's motto "Developing leaders who can change the world." I'm grateful for our relationship and many exchanges of stimulating ideas. I'm sure you'll share that feeling of gratitude when you read his book. It takes a lifetime of experiences, reflections, and research and synthesizes them into a very valuable manual for all organizations.

It's time to take happiness seriously.

Mohit Mukherjee
Founding Director
UPEACE Centre for Executive Education

INTRODUCTION

We need to talk about organizational happiness. We need happy organizations, happy people, and happy nations. A happy organization is a high-performing organization. Because a happy person is healthy and productive, the business case for organizational happiness is a "no-brainer."

So, even if you don't think ensuring happiness is part of your job as a leader, make it your responsibility because it's good business. Organizational happiness will be your competitive advantage—no doubt about it.

But I believe we need to look at people and organizations from a different perspective and recognize that for most people, "the pursuit of happiness" is very real and relevant—it's their life and it's our life.

I think part of an organization's role and responsibility is to facilitate and create an environment and leadership culture that makes happy employees. I don't think happiness is a private, individual thing. It's certainly a responsibility for our society and nations,[1] but organizations should take responsibility for the happiness of people, too—and not just as part of a corporate social responsibility strategy.

Organizational happiness can be difficult for some leaders and professionals to address. I find in my experience as an advisor and HR professional that we often find it easier to talk about "employee engagement," "motivation," or "staff satisfaction" than about "organizational

---

[1] The United Nations' Sustainable Development Goals are easily linked to happiness for individuals, organizations, and society.

happiness"—which from my perspective is what employee engagement, motivation, and staff satisfaction are all about.

The Happiness Sweet Spot and your Motivational Landscape—the frameworks and enabling tools in this book—give you a way to work with organizational happiness and employee engagement so that you have a competitive advantage. It is my hope that this will show you a compelling and easy path.

So why is it that you have not done this already?

As leaders, we experience an overflow of information. We get confused, and there are academic supporting arguments for any direction you might want to take or any decision you make. Right or left. Right or wrong.

I have seen this materialize in what I would call "paralyzed leadership." There is always doubt, a second opinion, and a reason to wait. We sit on our hands.

Making decisions is not easy. As a leader you have already delegated most of the decision-making, or your organization has already made the easy decisions.

That means you are left with the tough decisions—the ones that, if you seek advice or ask around, will always generate a "second opinion." This makes you lose power and speed.

At the same time, the world and the dynamics in our markets are moving so fast that if you don't move, you are toast.

Recent research[2] has shown that when you ask CEOs if they have doubts about making the right strategic decisions or doubt their own abilities to make the right people decisions, the number who say yes is rising dramatically with the speed of change and information (over)flow. When asked, "Do you ever doubt yourself?" in a

---

[2] *The CEO Report: Embracing the Paradoxes of Leadership and the Power of Doubt* (Heidrick and Struggles) is a good place to start if you want to dive into this subject.

2015 survey, 71 percent of the respondents said yes.

The paths to the future are made, not found.

To be successful, we need to turn strategy into action. Now. Fast.

I believe that as leaders, we need to be able to reduce complexity and use simple tools with simple rules[3] and heartfelt values and beliefs—so that we dare to lead.

The research, the academic work, and the case studies are already there. I want to give you a framework to work with organizational happiness: *the Happiness Sweet Spot.* And I will give you a way to measure, monitor, and follow up on organizational happiness and employee engagement. That is your *Motivational Landscape.*

---

[3] An inspiring book on this topic is *Simple Rules: How to Thrive in a Complex World* (2015) by Donald N. Sull and Kathleen M. Eisenhardt.

The Happiness Sweet Spot and your Motivational Landscape make up an enabling platform and a framework within which to work with organizational happiness, to operationalize your strategy, and to get you from strategy to action and behavior. It's simple, powerful, and fast. Some leaders call it "a strategy for people decision-making."

The Happiness Sweet Spot is a powerful and unique idea, because it presents what we already know in a simple model that works and is easily actionable. That's it!

Happiness as Organizational DNA

Happiness? At work? Are you kidding me?

For many leaders and organizations, happiness is an alien concept or a word that belongs in the "private sphere" of the individual employee. You can be happy at home.

But we are all in pursuit of happiness every day, and an exceptional energy is unleashed when we find the key to unlocking engagement and motivation and take happiness in our organization seriously.

Therefore I think it is time to start talking about organizational happiness as a real competitive advantage.

Sometimes we shy away from such a discussion because it is too "touchy-feely." It "feels" like it's not about business models, business cases, and organizational development. But it is exactly that. We shy away because we fear it makes us look too soft, unprofessional, or not serious enough to do real business.

Some organizations already take organizational happiness seriously and have a strategy for happiness. A well-known example is Zappos, an online shoe and clothing retailer based in Las Vegas, Nevada. Zappos has contributed on a large scale to building tangible business cases for happiness.[4]

Tony Hsieh, the author of *Delivering Happiness: A Path to Profits, Passion, and Purpose,* became involved with Zappos in 1999, about two months after the company was founded. Under his leadership, Zappos grew gross merchandise sales from $1.6 million in 2000 to more than $1 billion in 2008 by focusing relentlessly on customer service—and organizational happiness.

Like Hsieh, I think most organizations have an enormous potential to do better. And I think we should take organizational happiness

---

[4] Hsieh, Delivering Happiness.

seriously and talk about it as one of the top-three most important strategies for success in our organizations. Because it's the key to unlocking potential in the most effective way. It will give you a unique competitive advantage. And your business reasons for investing in organizational happiness are significant.

My own journey with taking happiness seriously really started in 2010 with an academic interest in the science of happiness in connection with implementing strategies for employee engagement. I started reading everything I could find on the topic.

In June 2011 the author Shawn Achor wrote an article for the *Harvard Business Review* titled "The Happiness Dividend," and in 2012 *HBR* dedicated an issue to happiness called The Value of Happiness.[5]

That really got me inspired, and I dived into the science of happiness with the purpose of

---

[5] *Harvard Business Review*, January/February 2012.

understanding it and helping organizations apply it in an operational way.

In 2014 Mohit Mukherjee[6] and I started an initiative called "Just Do Happy" to help facilitate ambitious organizations creating real strategies for organizational happiness. I also posted a LinkedIn article that year on "5 Reasons Why Happiness and Well-Being Will Be Relevant for You in 2015." It got a lot of attention in only a few days.

JUST DO HAPPY
taking happiness seriously.

That told me that leaders and organizational professionals were curious about the subject. But still, in 2014 organizational happiness was perceived and implemented as celebrating successes, doing a lot of high-fives, and having a soccer table in the office.

---

[6] Mukherjee is founding director of the UPEACE Centre for Executive Education in Costa Rica.

In 2015 we launched the Happiness Sweet Spot[7] to inspire leaders and organizations and offer a framework and a structure for working seriously with organizational happiness. This has allowed us to meet many amazing, inspiring people, and I have had the privilege of helping organizations work on making happiness a strategic part of creating a high-performing organization with a competitive advantage.

This work has generated multiple insights into developing tools and models for implementing strategies for organizational happiness.

We learned that happiness is in our organizational DNA. It means that we believe in happiness as the engine and driver for everything we do as an organization and everything we are. It's in our DNA.

The metaphorical term *organizational DNA* is based on the biological and chemical term *DNA*.

---

[7] See www.TheHappinessSweetSpot.com.

DNA is the molecule that encodes the genetic instructions in living organisms. Everything that a cell is and does comes from its DNA. The DNA informs and directs everything that happens to each cell in the body and through these cells directs what happens to the entire organism.

When we work with organizational happiness and employee engagement, the first question is "How do we do it?" That is the theme of this book.

The second question when we implement strategies is "How do we know if our strategy is working as intended?" Your yearly employee engagement survey will not tell you that. It's a snapshot of old data and not an up-to-date key performance indicator (KPI) of organizational happiness and employee engagement.

And a feeling is not enough. You can't rely on gut feelings only and out-of-date data when you make decisions about people and are monitoring one of your most important strategies for success.

Therefore, we developed a simple tool: Your Motivational Landscape measures happiness and engagement as a KPI for our partners on a regular basis (one to four times a month) with a pulse survey using ten simple and relevant questions.

MOTIVATIONAL
LANDSCAPE

We help you get a handle on employee engagement

At the end of the book is a list of resources that you can turn to for inspiration if you want to explore or dive into the science of happiness and the three pillars of the Happiness Sweet Spot. This literature and these cases have also served as background for this book.

CHAPTER 1

THE SCIENCE OF HAPPINESS

It's difficult to talk about organizational happiness without grounding it in some of the academic work and research that makes it legitimate to refer to happiness in organizations as a premise for high performance and success.

In the past two decades the study of emotion, emotional intelligence, and related topics has grown significantly.

One of the emotions that psychologists have studied most intensively is happiness. Organizational psychologists, economists, and neuroscientists have joined in learning more about it. These disciplines have distinct but intersecting interests: Psychologists want to understand what people feel, economists want to know what people value, and neuroscientists want to know how people's brains respond to rewards and so on. Having three separate disciplines all interested in a single topic has put that topic on the scientific map.

Papers on happiness are published in the journal *Science*, people who study happiness win Nobel Prizes, and governments all over the world are rushing to figure out how to measure and increase the happiness of their citizens.

Gross National Happiness (also known by the initialism GNH) is a philosophy that guides the government of Bhutan. It includes an index that is used to measure the collective happiness and well-being of a population. Gross National Happiness was instituted as the goal of Bhutan's government in the constitution of Bhutan enacted on 18 July 2008.

Also, in 2011, the UN General Assembly passed Resolution "Happiness: toward a holistic approach to development" urging member nations to follow the example of Bhutan and measure happiness and well-being and calling happiness a "fundamental human goal."

From an organizational point of view we are talking about "The Happiness Dividend,"[8] the Happiness Sweet Spot, and the business case for organizational happiness (chapters 2 and 3).

A lot of the research confirms things we already know or at least does not surprise us: People who are in good romantic relationships are happier than those who aren't. Healthy people are happier than sick people. People who participate in their community are happier than those who don't. Rich people are happier than poor people. And so on.

Why is this interesting for organizations? Because happy people are more creative and more productive.

In the introduction I promised that this book would be a guide from strategy to action, so I will not spend a lot of time on the academics. I will just conclude that the science of happiness is a real thing. And it makes sense for individuals,

---

[8] Achor, "The Happiness Dividend."

organizations, and nations to pursue happiness, because it leads to wealth, health, innovation, and productivity.

All that means that there is a great case to be made for organizational happiness in business. But also, we simply need more happy people and happy societies on our earth, in my opinion. It will make a better world.

And you have a sweet spot right there.

Happiness serves all.
Source: Lars Kure Juul

It is good from three perspectives.

This universal sweet spot is not the subject of this book. The universal happiness sweet spot is for policy makers and corporate social responsibility professionals.

My focus and mission is to make it happen in organizations—to go from strategy to action. From words to behavior.

For that, a good, simple model is the PERMA model, developed by Martin Seligman.

The five elements of the PERMA model can help people reach a life of fulfillment, happiness, and meaning. I will use that model as a scientific reference for building your organizational happiness strategy and establishing your Motivational Landscape. The model can be applied to organizations when we know the correlation between happiness and employee engagement and performance.

The organizational perspective is what we offer with the Happiness Sweet Spot framework and the three pillars of organizational happiness.

I describe the model in detail in chapter 3, but in short, it establishes that happiness in organizations happens when a heartfelt purpose, strengths-based leadership, and a culture of compassion come together in a sweet spot where the full potential of the organization is unleashed.

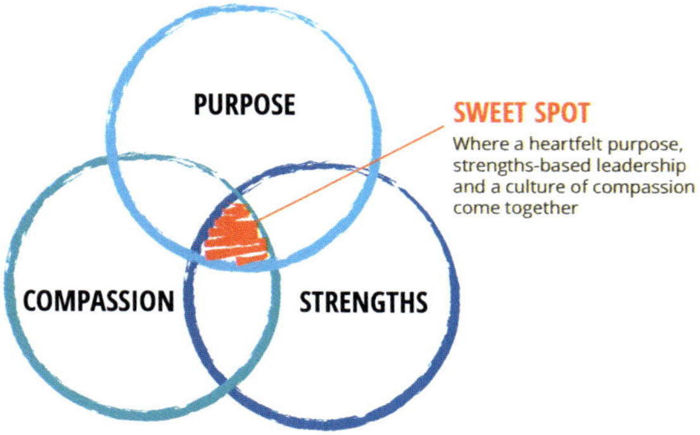

The PERMA Model

Psychologist Dr. Martin Seligman, widely viewed as the father of positive psychology, asserts that happiness (he also uses the terms *well-being* and *flourishing*) is about five elements, which can be captured by the acronym PERMA:

- Positive emotions—feeling good
- Engagement—being completely absorbed in activities
- Relationships—being authentically connected to others
- Meaning—purposeful existence
- Achievement—a sense of accomplishment and success

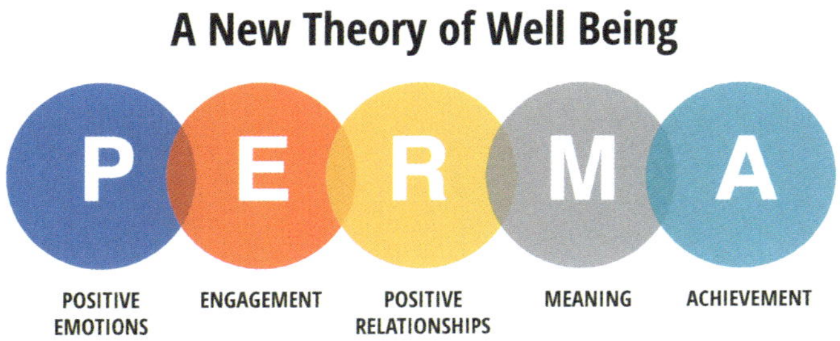

He describes and elaborates on the model in his 2011 book *Flourish*.[9]

Martin Seligman's research and case studies are relevant in an organizational context.

In the next section, I elaborate a bit more in depth on each of the five areas.

People are still people when they go to work. And we saw from research that happy employees perform better and produce better results. So, it is quite interesting to dive into what makes people happy and put it in an organizational context. That is what we do in the Happiness Sweet Spot model.

Positive Emotions

Focusing on positive emotions is about how to create an environment that enables

- time for self-reflection;
- sharing of experiences (and knowledge);

[9] Seligman, *Flourish*.

- a sense of belonging and connectedness (to individuals, the team, and the organization); and
- feelings of joy, hope, and contentment.

Positive emotions help facilitate a change in mind-set and are conducive to building trust, teamwork, and a feeling of oneness.

Engagement

Engagement is about giving all employees the opportunity to fully participate in the direction the team wants to go by

- connecting it with your own and the organization's purpose or "why";
- building on strengths and strengths-based leadership;
- creating a feeling of psychological safety that enables the building of a productive environment, where all have a feeling of being heard and can contribute to solutions; and
- facilitating greater collaboration and a sense of "We are a team" culture.

Relationships

We will look at how to move beyond job titles and see unique individuals. Relationships act as an engine for success by

- catalyzing the strengths of the individuals and the dynamic of their team relationships;
- creating connections beyond people's professional roles, encouraging greater connectedness and a desire to support and encourage each other; and
- fostering a willingness to go the "extra mile" for the team and individual team members.

Meaning

Meaning is about joining and blending—resonating with—the purpose of an individual with that of the team, and ultimately with the purpose of the organization. Meaning

- is more than the answer to "What's my job?"
- is entwined with purpose—both the organizational purpose and the personal *why* of our employees; and

- leads to asking, "How can I add value?" while feeling challenged and having a sense of working toward a common goal for a higher purpose.

Achievement

Recognizing successes is about

- appreciating that the success of the individual feeds the success of the team;
- setting goals and communicating clearly about them;
- identifying collective targets;
- being aware of the implications for each individual;
- realizing that when we support each other, we each have success; and
- knowing that it adds to the momentum of change and creates value.

These five elements can help people reach a life of fulfillment, happiness, and meaning. Whether at work or in another setting, people need to feel good, engage, belong, understand *why*, and make a difference. This makes sense and is something we can work with in an organizational context. And we already know from science—including economists' statistics—that it leads to high performance and great results.

The organizational perspective is what we offer with the Happiness Sweet Spot framework and the three pillars of organizational happiness.

Later in the book, I use the PERMA model as a scientific reference to help you build your organizational happiness strategy and establish your Motivational Landscape.

First, I will dig deeper into and explore the business reasons for making organizational happiness a priority.

CHAPTER 2

THE BUSINESS CASE AND THE RECIPE FOR ORGANIZATIONAL HAPPINESS

The business case for working with organizational happiness and employee engagement is not difficult to build. In this chapter I will help you explore all the "whys" and look at the figures based on research and cases, and you will learn how to build your own business case based on relevant key performance indicators (KPIs).

"Nice idea—feels good. *Show me the business case!*"

As an HR executive and trusted advisor, I often get that kind of response when we introduce ideas for new organizational development activities.

I think it's a good test and challenge to evaluate whether we're using our money wisely and investing in the right strategic initiatives.

So, hands down, what's the business argument for organizational happiness and using the Happiness Sweet Spot model to work strategically with organizational happiness? And how do we build a simple business case for happiness that everybody will understand and that becomes a "no-brainer" even for the CFO?

As a starting point we need to establish the fundamentals: Happy employees perform better, are more committed, and attract committed and talented people to the organization. They are healthier and take fewer sick days. They don't quit easily, they treat customers better, and they tend to be less stressed. Those are just a few relevant organizational and people measures that would easily build your business case in a concrete way.

From a market point of view, we take happiness seriously, because if we don't, we will be outperformed.[10] Using organizational happiness as a competitive advantage means that you are able to attract, develop, and retain the best talent in your industry. And the individual and team performance will be in the upper 10 percent of your industry. If you evaluate the success of your company based on market value, "human capital" and "intangible assets" are critical.[11]

---

[10] See, among others, Meghan Biro at http://www.forbes.com/sites/meghanbiro/2014/01/19/happy-employees-hefty-profits/.

[11] For inspiration on this I highly recommend Great People Decisions: Why They Matter So Much, Why They Are So Hard, and How You Can Master Them, by Claudio Fernández-Aráoz.

The most important competitive advantage is your ability to attract and retain top talent. In that sense organizational happiness will be a differentiator for you, as well as a competitive advantage.

The demographic challenges of the twenty-first century are making this competitive advantage even more relevant.

The changes in the makeup of our population, as a result of aging and migration, are hot topics in the media and the world of politics—and rightly so, because there is hardly a policy area that is not being affected by demographic change.

As organizational leaders we should be aware of how these challenges will affect our ability to attract resources and hire employees with the superpowers we need.

We all want to work for organizations that are oozing happiness. But what do they look like? I believe organizations are happy because they have a strong heartfelt purpose, believe in strengths-based leadership, and are cultivating a culture of compassion. Those are the three pillars in the Happiness Sweet Spot model.

Below is a collection of quantified and quantifiable benefits of focusing on organizational happiness and employee engagement. The figures are drawn from research by Gallup, Martin Seligman, Tom Rath, Shawn Achor, and other thought leaders and experts in this area.[12][13][14][15]

Figures are also based on our experience with implementing an organizational happiness strategy in organizations and working strategically with employee engagement.

---

[12] Research and cases by and from Gallup, Shawn Achor, Martin Seligman, and many more, including our own organizational development cases.

[13] Aaker, Leslie, and Schifrin, "The Business Case for Happiness."

[14] Marks, The Happiness Manifesto.

[15] Happiness Works: https://www.happinessatworksurvey.com/business-case.

There is a clear and evident trend in the research and the cases we know about:

- increased **performance and productivity**, 8–18 percent
- higher **customer satisfaction** and loyalty, 2–10 percent
- lower **employee turnover**, 6–73 percent
- higher **employee retention**
- lower number of sick leaves and less absenteeism, 7–37 percent
- more **innovation**, up to 300 percent
- higher **employee engagement**, 4–23 percent
- increased **profit**, 14–29 percent
- fewer **safety incidents**, 23–59 percent
- increased **sales**, 10–19 percent
- reduced **stress and burnout**, up to 400 percent
- better **quality**: fewer defects and errors, 6–27 percent
- increased ability to **drive change** / adaptability to change
- **customer loyalty**
- **ideas** for reducing cost-base

The figures represent the range for which I could find evidence in the research, cases, and our experience with organizational happiness implementation.

I don't think the exact figures are important. What is important are the figures for you and your organization.

Many of the figures are of course interrelated and highly dependent on how you measure, what you measure, and how clearly you are able to isolate the relevant cause and effect of your organizational happiness initiatives.

There is a clear correlation between your effort (defined as having a prioritized strategy with investments behind activities) and the outcome. The more you integrate your happiness strategy into your organization, the more value you create. Or, the more you integrate it, the better the business case.

The idea of including the benefit list is not to guarantee that your results will be the same as those on the list. Organizations are too complex for me to give you a single practice to copy, and as stated, there is a clear correlation between how you design your strategy, the investments you make, and the results you get.

But even with all the reservations about specific outcome, I would not be afraid to do a no-cure-no-pay agreement on implementing an organizational happiness strategy at any organization.

The aim of this section is to emphasize the business case and highlight the potentially short return on investment (ROI) you can have with organizational happiness strategies.

You will get your own results and own figures, depending on your unique circumstances and potential—and the way you approach your strategy in this area.

Make your own business case. Even a conservative one will make your CFO happy.

Your Business Case

Try to build a quick, very conservative business case on the back of a napkin, like this:

- How many employees do you have in your organization?
- What's your salary budget for this year?
- What's your projected employee turnover for this year?
- Calculate a 2 percent productivity increase. (That means you can save resources or do "more with less.")
- Calculate reduced sick leave of one or two days per year per employee. (That will reduce the cost of using contractors, stress-related expenses, and so on.)
- Calculate your retention rate up or calculate a reduction in turnover by 10–15 percent. (This figure will affect the costs of hiring, knowledge gaps, onboarding, and so on.)

When I do a rough calculation for an organization I'm working with at the moment that has five hundred employees, I get a result of close to $2 million. This represents profit and cost reductions combined.

The ROI in this case takes less than three months. My experience with investments to drive your organizational happiness strategy is that very often the implementation of the strategy is about focusing and aiming the investments you are already making around your people strategy, training and development, and so on. It's usually not a huge extra investment.

And this is a very conservative business case. When we are able to unlock the potential in the organization, so that employees are playing to their strengths, feeling the purpose, and engaged and motivated, the actual productivity increase is a lot higher than 2 percent. Some studies suggest 28 percent on average.

On top of that, you should add the benefits of more innovation, more sustainable results, better customer service, higher customer satisfaction, unlocking and releasing management resources, and removing organizational inertia in general.

Those things are more difficult to put into a hard-core business case, but they are highly relevant and would make the case much more attractive.

It is fair to say that this conservative business case for working strategically with organizational happiness is solid. And the potential and real value is a lot more than that.

Would that make you or your CEO—or CFO—want to take happiness seriously in your organization?

Yes.

The Recipe

Before we jump in and explore each of the elements in the Happiness Sweet Spot and your Motivational Landscape, I'll give you the five steps here and revert to it when we work on the recipe for your organization within the framework of the Happiness Sweet Spot.

Five easy steps to organizational happiness and a fully charged organization

1. Find a framework that works for you. This book is an example of a framework.
2. Make the assessment; know your organization.
3. Do your business case.
4. Base your "strategy-to-action-plan" on
    i. purpose—your why,
    ii. strengths-based leadership, and
    iii. compassion.
5. Measure, review, and follow up—make it stick!

The next five chapters will give you insight, research, and background information on all the elements of the Recipe for Organizational Happiness.

CHAPTER 3

THE HAPPINESS SWEET SPOT

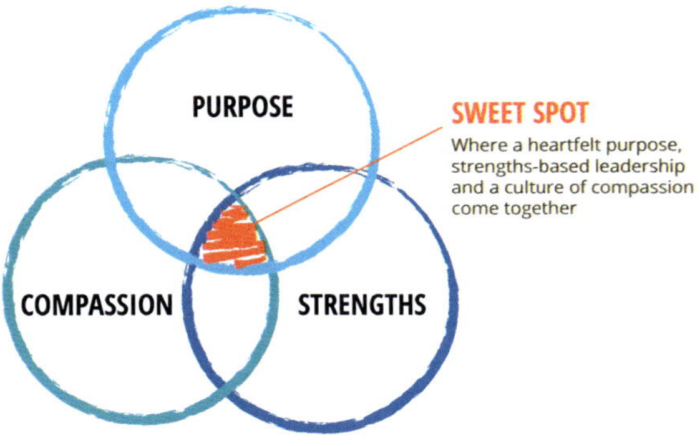

Now we have come to the "how." In my work with organizational happiness and employee engagement I have realized that three areas are especially conducive to catalyzing happiness and employee engagement. It's about how organizations cultivate a culture of compassion, *why* they are here, and how they lead and manage people. I will use this as the point of departure for working strategically with organizational happiness as an engine for high performance and sustainable results.

To work strategically with happiness in your organization, you need to break it down and develop strategies and facilitate actions in three main areas:

1. Purpose
2. Strengths
3. Compassion

We use the term *the three pillars of organizational happiness.* I will explain and elaborate on each of these as we go forward.

So, what is the Happiness Sweet Spot? You're in the Organizational Happiness Sweet Spot when you've found the place where your strategies and efforts around purpose, strengths-based leadership, and cultivating a culture of compassion come together, support one another, and are integrated.

When you ignite the sweet spot and, as leader, unlock the potential of the organization, your organization will be "fully charged."

Purpose

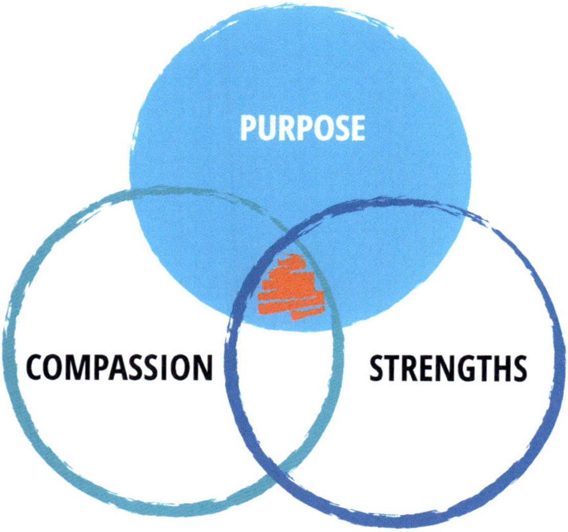

The first pillar of organizational happiness is purpose.

Purpose is your organizational *why*.

It's a heartfelt "reason for being" that is bigger than profit. When market conditions are right, companies can be successful with a pure profit purpose. But a lot of potential is released when it's more than that.

When your purpose is clear, many other things get easier: your storytelling to customers about why to buy, attracting the best people to your organization, and more.

On the individual level your *why* brings meaning, which is the M in the PERMA model I introduced earlier.

When it is really good, your organizational *why* resonates—does not conflict—with the personal *why* of the people in the organization.

- Purpose brings meaning.
- Having a purpose is a competitive advantage.
- Your purpose is your employer brand.

And you need a strong purpose to attract and retain top talent. If you don't have that, your organization will struggle and not last.

For some organizations a heartfelt purpose and *why* comes easily and naturally. For other organizations it is a bit of a stretch to come up with a "meaningful" purpose.

Scandinavian Tobacco Group's promise is "We create moments of great enjoyment for smokers."[16]

The PepsiCo mission statement is as follows: "Our mission is to be the world's premier consumer products company focused on convenient foods and beverages. We seek to produce financial rewards to investors as we provide opportunities for growth and enrichment to our employees, our business partners and the communities in which we operate. And in everything we do, we strive for honesty, fairness and integrity."[17]

The mission statement of Patagonia is as follows: "Build the best product, cause no

---

[16] www.st-group.com/en/our-company.

[17] http://www.pepsico.com. The mission statement is from 2013.

unnecessary harm, use business to inspire and implement solutions to the environmental crisis."[18]

Which one would you like to give your best to? What company would get the best part of you? Which company would you talk about with pride at a cocktail party?

For Scandinavian Tobacco Group and PepsiCo, my best guess is that they have to attract top talent with a promise of exceptional professional development, above industry salary, and retain talent with contractual bindings. This can be a successful strategy, but it's really hard work—not heart work.

Of course that would depend on the actions and actual behavior those companies put behind their statements.

But the stronger and more heartfelt the purpose, the easier it is for employees to give all

---

[18] https://www.patagonia.com/company-info.html.

they have, to want to work there, to relate to and be proud of it. It makes us happy on a personal level. In chapter 4, I will unpack and elaborate further on purpose.

Strengths

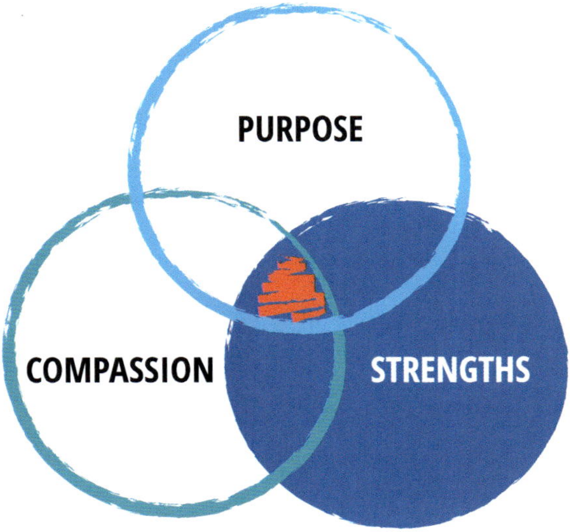

The second pillar of organizational happiness is strengths-based leadership and real talent management. That means discovering people's talents, strengths, and potential and putting them into play for your organization.

Focusing on strengths and what's working well will result in the highest employee engagement.

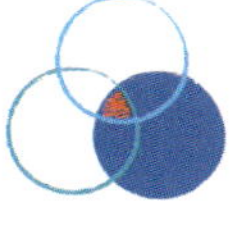

- Conversations about strengths reveal the superpowers in an organization.
- Effective talent management recognizes that everybody has talent, potential, and strengths.
- Strengths-based leadership unlocks an organization's potential.
- A successful talent management strategy requires simple processes and enabling tools.

It's no surprise to you as a leader that ignorance results in the lowest engagement. A focus on problems and what's not working, with a fix-it attitude, leads to higher engagement. But it's not nearly as high as the engagement that is stimulated by a strengths-based leader.

In chapter 5, I will give you an understanding of how to lead your organization from a strengths-based perspective to build the second pillar of the Happiness Sweet Spot.

Compassion

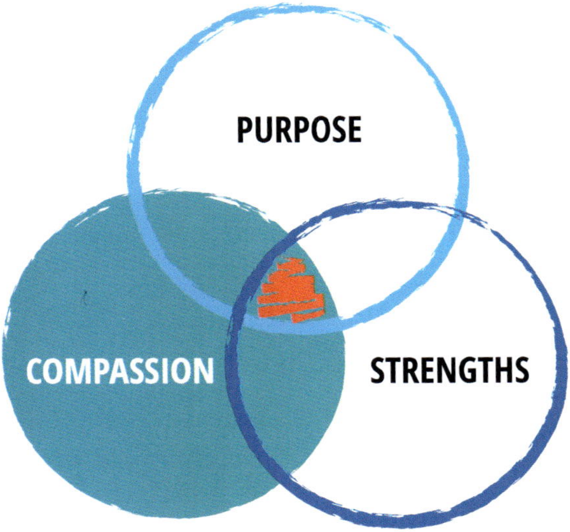

The third pillar of organizational happiness is cultivating a culture of compassion. It means people are interested in understanding the difficulties of other people and have a burning desire to help them.

- Compassion and curiosity increase employee loyalty and trust.

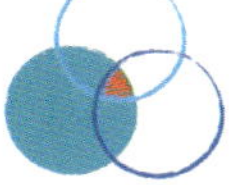

- Compassion boosts team performance by helping employees feel "safe."
- Compassion facilitates the spirit of experimentation and is critical for creativity.

The way I see it, compassion is about leadership and leadership is about compassion. If you aspire to be an effective leader, you can't do it successfully without compassion.

Research has demonstrated that even before establishing their own credibility or competence, leaders who project warmth are more effective than those who lead with toughness. Compassion, kindness, and warmth accelerate trust, which is a building block for performance and teamwork.

This third and last pillar of the Happiness Sweet Spot is unpacked and explored in chapter 6.

When you work with the three pillars of organizational happiness as an engine for sustainable success, you need to know if you've hit the sweet spot for your organization. Do you put the right emphasis on each of the pillars? What works best for your unique situation in your organization? Are your efforts paying off?

Knowing your Motivational Landscape will help you determine whether you're on the right track.

Your Motivational Landscape

MOTIVATIONAL LANDSCAPE

We help you get a handle on employee engagement

If you work strategically with organizational happiness as an engine for sustainable success, you need to know if you are within the sweet spot.

We have developed a simple tool that will help you keep an eye on this.

You need to know, How are we doing right now?

Because you wouldn't and can't rely on gut feelings alone.

Your Motivational Landscape is a simple pulse survey and tool that tells you about the state of your organizational happiness and employee engagement—in real time.

The tool is connected to the three pillars in the Happiness Sweet Spot, so you can measure, monitor, and follow up on your activities and purpose, strengths, and compassion.

Your Motivational Landscape is built on research and case studies on what creates and is conducive to organizational happiness, employee engagement, and high performance. Behind the scenes we have built in the PERMA model and the science of happiness, because they are fundamental to this.

It consists of ten unique questions related to organizational happiness and employee engagement, asked on a regular basis. The results are reported on a dashboard and provide important data your business depends on for its success.

The 10 Questions in Your Motivational Landscape

1. I feel happy at work.

PURPOSE

2. I'm proud of being part of my organization.
3. I know how I contribute to the mission of our organization.
4. I would recommend a friend for a job here.

STRENGTHS

5. I have the opportunity to do what I do best.
6. I have opportunities to learn, grow, and develop.
7. I have the resources available that enable me to do a good job.

COMPASSION

8. I feel people care about me.
9. I get recognition or praise (I am appreciated).
10. My opinion counts.

Every question is accompanied by an optional link where employees can elaborate by responding to these two prompts:

- What worked well?
- It would be even better if...

Your Motivational Landscape platform will also engage employees in the pursuit of organizational happiness. Happiness needs to be on the agenda and in conversations at the lunch table and the cocktail party.

Innocent or Excellent?

To develop a culture of organizational happiness that evokes emotions in your employees, you can't simply copy policies and practices from another organization or from a book and framework like this one.

Knowing about them is inspiring and helpful, but yours must be consciously designed for your organization:

1. Where are we now?
2. What works here, now?

In other words, "Start where you are. Use what you have. Do what you can."[19]

To help you determine and reflect on where your organization is now as a point of departure for your strategy, we have designed a simple framework around the Happiness Sweet Spot to evaluate whether the people in your organization are inexperienced or excellent at understanding

---

[19] Tennis player Arthur Ashe.

and cultivating a sense of purpose, strengths, and compassion.[20]

Think about your team or organization and ask yourself these questions for reflection:

- What are its characteristics?
- Do you have a heartfelt purpose that resonates with the *why* of the people in your organization?
- Are you focused on building a strong leadership culture?
- Do you cultivate a culture of compassion?
- Do you have a talent management strategy that recognizes that everybody in the organization has talent, potential, and strengths?

Think about this as you—mentally or at TheHappinessSweetSpot.com—place the marker on the scale below somewhere between zero and 100 as it relates to the purpose, compassion, and talent in your organization.

---

[20] See www.thehappinesssweetspot.com/assessment/.

MOTIVATIONAL LANDSCAPE

We help you get a handle on employee engagement

Besides your own (or your team's) assessment based on your knowledge of and experience in your organization, a way to fast track, or get a clear picture, is to start taking advantage of the features in Motivational Landscape.[21]

You could pick a relevant group of people who are representative of your organization, set them up in the system, and have your preliminary sweet spot score and detailed scores on purpose, strengths, and compassion within a few days.

That's a strong point of departure for choosing the right strategy for you related to

---

[21] The website www.MotivationalLandscape.com includes access to a free trial.

organizational happiness and employee engagement.

Now is the time to dive into the *how* and *why* of each of the three pillars of organizational happiness.

In chapter 7, I elaborate on how to establish your Motivational Landscape and offer you a way to measure, monitor, and follow up on your organizational happiness strategy.

In the next chapters, I will lead you through a deeper understanding of the three pillars of organizational happiness and how to work with them, and explore why they are so important.

CHAPTER 4

PURPOSE

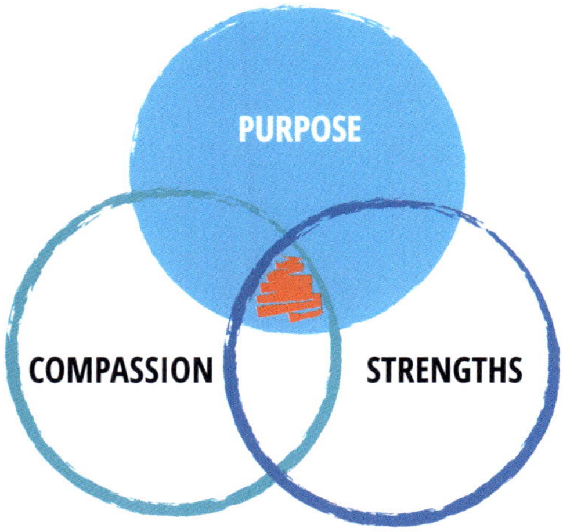

The first pillar of organizational happiness

Purpose is your organization's *why*—a heartfelt "reason for being" that is bigger than profit and resonates with the personal *why* of the people in the organization.

Purpose brings meaning. And meaning is conducive to organizational happiness and employee engagement. As an organization you need a purpose—a *why*—that is bigger and stronger than making money for your shareholders or "being the best in our industry."

Many experts, thinkers, thought leaders, authors, and practitioners—myself included—have an opinion about what really works and how best to approach working with your organizational purpose and organizational *why*.

These three men are sources of great inspiration and have profound insight in this area:

1. Simon Sinek[22]
2. Robert E. Quinn[23]
3. Martin Seligman[24]

In this chapter I have quoted these thinkers where appropriate. Most of the content about purpose, strengths, and compassion is not from my research or a new "invention." The academic foundation and research is already there.

I'm inspired by the best researchers and thought leaders, and I use my practical experience and my "superpower" to "see" what really works.

---

[22] Visit www.StartWithWhy.com or watch Sinek's famous TED talk from 2009, "Start with Why: How Great Leaders Inspire Action."

[23] Quinn is the author of many books and articles on leadership and purpose. A place to start is "Creating a Purpose-Driven Organization" from the July–August 2018 issue of *Harvard Business Review*.

[24] Seligman is a strong promoter within the scientific community of his theories of positive psychology and well-being. See also the PERMA model in chapter 1.

I am a practitioner and thought leader on organizational happiness and employee engagement. And my mission here is to share what I know works.

First a little personal story on purpose and *why*.

I was part of the executive management team in an international company in the construction industry that made building materials.

My role was as director for the Nordic and Baltic regions, and I was responsible for human resources, organization, communication, and operational excellence.

The organizational mission and vision were "to create sustainable growth and create value."

We invested in and worked hard on values, branding, and leadership development. And it was a nice place to be, in the sense that we were financially successful, there was room for development, and we were launching some cool initiatives in my area of responsibility. Professionally I was thriving and learning, and I liked my colleagues. I felt like I made a difference every day.

But for what? It was really all about being more profitable than the last period, in order to make more profit for the shareholders. That was it! And on top of that, we were not very environmentally friendly, to put it diplomatically.

When I had time off and could think and reflect, I realized there was an imbalance between what I was working for and my personal values and the way I otherwise lived my life.

I was trying to tell myself and communicate as a company brand that we helped build houses that didn't collapse over your head. (This was around the time when Haiti was devastated by a catastrophic earthquake, in 2010.)

But I was lying—to myself and to others. Because the true mission of the company was to make money for the shareholders. And from a professional point of view, I had great difficulty accepting that we were not able to unlock the full potential of the organization with a purpose that was crafted to make a profit for the shareholders. The purpose wasn't meaningful. It was frustrating.

It was difficult to drive a change toward a more heartfelt purpose, because in financial terms the company was successful. So what was the real issue? What was the problem?

Maybe it was *my* problem? I couldn't get my heart into it!

I'm convinced we could have done much more with that organization in terms of high performance and delivering sustainable results if we had been brave and willing enough to develop a story and a purpose that was about more than profit.

In the end I had to tell my chairman that—that I couldn't get my heart into it and would have to leave when we had hired a suitable successor.

He said, "I want to kill you." I took that as a compliment and a sign of loyalty, a job well done, and the good personal connection between us.

This is an example of a purpose that didn't bring meaning or spark emotions—in me and in many others in the company. Some stayed and some left. But I believe that all of them had more in them than what the company could turn into performance and results.

Think about it: What's a better motivator than a genuine belief that the work we do matters? And what's more human than seeking a sense of meaning in the work we do? Employees are increasingly looking for a sense of purpose—and you should too, if you want to build a competitive advantage and organizational happiness.

I have also had positions with NGOs whose purposes and missions are as follows:

> *"We fight poverty by helping the poor to fight for their rights and break the structures, which holds them back in hunger and poverty."*

or

> *"We inspire and empower everyone to take action against food waste."*

Those organizations got the best parts of me, in terms of my hard work, engagement, and dedication, even though the paycheck showed a third or a fourth of what I could have made if I had put my heart into a traditional management consulting company or a successful company in the building materials industry.

Not everyone thinks, feels, and acts like me, but most of us are willing to give more and demand less for a good heartfelt purpose. Then it becomes "heart work."

I have never seen harder-working employees, accepting very difficult working conditions, than those in the NGO world, because we were working for something bigger than ourselves, something important.

Sometimes I also use the Coca-Cola Company as an example. Their purpose is to sell Coca-Cola. We know that. But their storytelling is about humanity, sharing, and contributing to society. They know the power of purpose.

So let's dig deeper into why working with organizational purpose makes such a difference.

Why Purpose?

Purpose brings meaning. Meaning is a building block of happiness and one of the advantages of creating organizational happiness.

Researchers in the science of happiness say that it is almost impossible to be happy without a purpose.

In the Happiness Sweet Spot we define purpose as your organization's *why*—a heartfelt "reason for being" that is bigger than profit and resonates with the personal *why* of the people in the organization. Purpose brings meaning. Meaning is essential for motivation, engagement, and individual happiness.

We talk about having "a sense of purpose." It's that feeling that leads to meaning, motivation, and engagement, and leads to higher performance.

Purpose in what you do provides a sense of fulfillment and is the most significant factor enabling you to be at your best.

Purpose allows you to get through hard times and to persevere through adversity.

Purpose acts like a True North in directing your thoughts, feelings, and behavior.

Purpose gives motivation and guides you in achieving your authentic potential.

Having a sense of purpose significantly benefits your health, work performance, and happiness—or *flourishing*, as Martin Seligman would say.

In early 2018 the EY Beacon Institute surveyed nearly 1,500 leaders from around the world. The results[25] revealed how best-in-class purposeful companies are using their purpose as a beacon to navigate turbulent times—as well as

---

[25] https://www.ey.com/en_gl/purpose.

how they are embedding their purpose in decisions and daily actions throughout their organizations. We asked them whether their companies have a sense of purpose, what that means to them, and what value it provides in our volatile world.

More than 70 percent of the leaders said they believe that integrating a sense of purpose into their business helps them navigate this era of disruption.

The majority of leaders (two-thirds) said they are rethinking what purpose means to them and their organization today.

And of those two-thirds, more than half are adopting a purpose that goes beyond shareholder value and toward a more socially engaged purpose that creates value for "a broad set of stakeholders."

In other words, they're building or developing a purpose that serves the wider world—one that is bigger than profit.

Having a well-integrated purpose will help your organization navigate disruption and catalyze high performance, contributing to organizational happiness.

Some of the benefits of having a clear purpose and *why*:

- Higher customer loyalty
- Better brand value and reputation
- Ability to attract and retain top talent
- Ability to develop innovative new products and services

What's not to like?

But how do you find and develop a clear purpose and a strong *why*?

I think some of the best and most inspiring work done on purpose and finding your *why* is by Simon Sinek.

Although Simon Sinek did not invent purpose or *why*, I think he has been able to capture the idea of purpose as a driving force for individuals and organizations in a way that is simple, easy to understand, and operational.

We will get back to the *how*, but before we dive into models and actions, I think we need to elaborate a bit on our purpose as private individuals and our purpose at work. And how they resonate or don't.

Because who says that everyone should get their purpose and *why* from their job?

The question here is, "How far can and should you go to align yourself with your organization's *why* and the personal *whys* of your employees?"

My personal purpose and *why* is "to inspire, facilitate, and help, so that people and organizations with important missions develop, aspire, and succeed."

Behind my purpose and *why* are the personal values and guiding principles that I live by:

- Effect
- Playfulness
- Love

I'm privileged to live a life where I live and breathe my purpose in my professional life and most of my life is in sync with my personal values.

But, while we are addressing and highlighting the importance of a clear, heartfelt organizational purpose and *why*, I think it is important to recognize and respect that employees have different motivations for going to work every day.

It's good if your organizational purpose and the personal *why* of your employees and colleagues are in total alignment. But the reality is that this is very difficult and sometimes impossible. A motivation for going to work might be "I need to feed my family" or "I work so I can live" or "I need to pay for my children's education." In these cases, it is good enough to "not be in conflict." The motivation is still genuine and authentic.

What I often see happening for people working for organizations with a strong purpose is what you could call an "acquired mission" or a "purpose journey." You meet an organization—or, typically, a leader—that is attractive to you, gradually learn about the purpose, and take a journey with the organization until you are aligned, or living the purpose.

With some organizations I work with, this can happen almost before you know it, in the sense that you get pulled in when you start to understand the magnitude of the difference you can make as an organization that serves a really important purpose or mission.[26]

So, we need to accept that alignment is best but that "not being in conflict" can also be good. Employees might be on a "purpose journey" with

---

[26] UPEACE, the Child Cancer Association, and Too Good To Go are recent examples for me.

our organization, or our organizational purpose may never be fully aligned with that of some employees. As long as there is no conflict, it's OK.

You can resonate without being in total alignment.

If your personal values and *why* are in conflict with the purpose of the organization you're working for, like in my case above, you need to do something about it. Or your leader should help you do something about it. We all deserve to work in a place where we can be motivated and engaged. That does not happen when your values and *why* are in conflict with the culture at work.

You can create and establish organizational happiness and happy employees without a total alignment.

When I say the organizational *why* should *resonate* with the *why* of your employees, it means that the *whys* have the same vibration; they can go hand in hand without having to be the same. It can also mean that the *why* is received and reflected by your employees to make it even stronger. There is and should be a connection.

When we want to work with organizational happiness and employee engagement, our role as leaders and professionals is to create an organizational frame and environment where the tone is “We know we are ignited by purpose and *why*, and we respect differences.”

This “purpose-inclusive” approach will be conducive to a sense of pride, a desire to contribute, and a sense of oneness and being part of a team.

A clear organizational *why* enables you to attract and retain talent and makes employees proud of working for you.

How To

As a context for working with and understanding the power of *why*, I want to share a simple framework based on Simon Sinek's idea from his 2009 TED talk "Start with Why," in which he presented what he calls the Golden Circle.

When I asked Simon Sinek about sharing and presenting his idea and some of the material around "Start with Why"[27] in this book, he responded, "I appreciate your willingness to help us spread the message to inspire others. You are more than welcome. The whole idea of this message is to share it with as many people as possible. We cannot do that alone and are grateful for you being part of the movement to inspire that is helping us spread this idea to live in service to others...Stay inspired. Inspire others."

And I thought, *Here is a man who lives his* why. I have great respect for that.

---

[27] https://startwithwhy.com.

Sinek was and is interested in why some leaders and organizations are able to inspire greater loyalty and higher engagement in relation to customers and employees.

He found that most organizations function by focusing on the following:

1. *What* we do
2. *How* we do it
3. *Why* we do it

That goes for our own professional lives as well. It's how we tell our story at the dinner table or cocktail party.

When those three areas are aligned, it gives us a filter through which to make decisions, choose our behavior, and connect with customers and our current and future employees.

This provides a basis for innovation and for building trust and is crucial to employee engagement, well-functioning teams, high performance, and…organizational happiness.

When all three areas are in balance, others will say, "We know who you are," "We know what you stand for."

The simple idea is the Golden Circle:

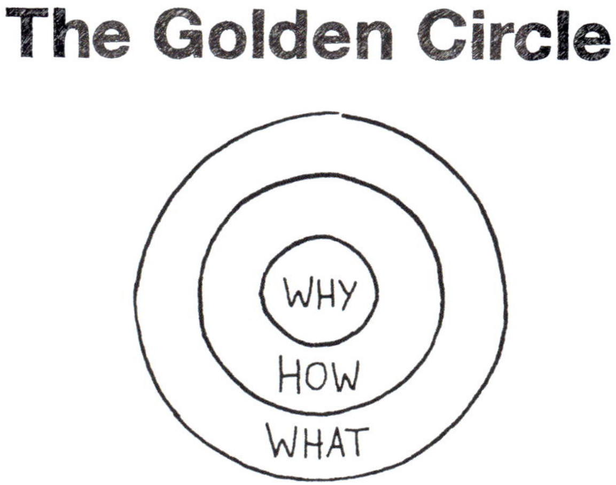

Every organization and person knows *what* they do.

For an organization, *what* refers to the products they sell or the services they offer. For a person, it is their job title or role.

Some organizations and people know *how* they do what they do. We call it our "competitive advantage," "unique selling proposition," or "special sauce." It reflects our strengths, values, culture, and guiding principles.

These are the things we think make us different from our colleagues and competitors in the market—what make us special or different from everyone else.

Very few people and very few organizations can clearly articulate *why* they do what they do. *Why* is a purpose, a cause, or a belief.

The *why* provides a clear answer to the questions, "Why do you get out of bed every morning?" "Why does your organization exist?" and "Why should that matter to anyone else?"

The *why* is about our contribution toward affecting and serving others. The *why* inspires us. It can even make us cry.

Making money is not a *why*. Revenues, profits, salaries, and other monetary measurements are results of what we do.

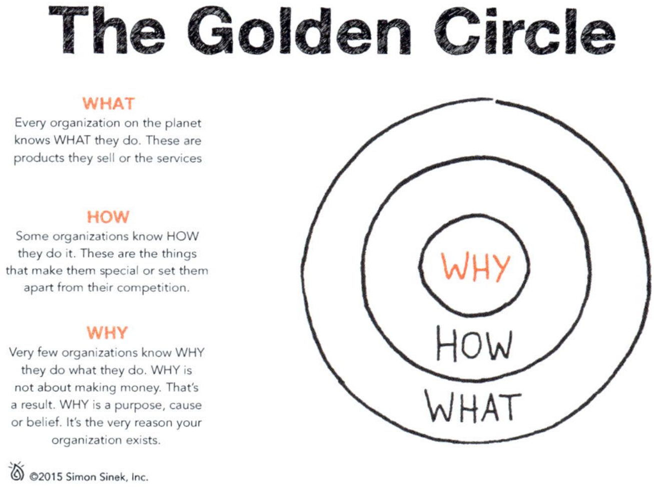

When you look at this model, you see that organizations and people naturally communicate from the outside in.

We typically go from what is easiest to understand to what is hardest to understand and explain.

We tell people *what* we do. We tell them *how* we are different or better. And then we expect a behavior like a purchase, a vote, or support.

The challenge is that *what* and *how* do not really inspire action or changes in behavior. Facts and figures make rational sense, but we and our customers do not make decisions based purely on facts and figures.

Starting with *what* is what commodities do.

Starting with your *why* is what leaders do. Leaders inspire.

And organizations with a clear and loud *why* that serves and is more than a financial measure have loyal customers and employees. And are able to attract the best people.

Leaders and organizations with the capacity to inspire start with their *why*—their passion, their reason for being. It's not a figure, a quick fix, or a product.

Think about it. What would you say at the dinner table or at a cocktail party when people asked you what you do and you started with "My passion is..."?

As a trusted advisor and management consultant, I meet a lot of leaders who have called me because they have a challenge, a problem, or an opportunity in relation to organizational development, leadership, or talent management. And they need my advice and help.

In my experience, I have learned that you cannot listen to a leader for thirty minutes and then give them a solution or suggest a quick fix for their problem. Sometimes that's what is expected of me, and it can be tempting to put on the expert hat and hand out a solution. But organizational development is never like that. If you aren't careful, you can be perceived as arrogant. And no one wants that.

If you are brave enough to say, "I don't know, but let's find out—together," you have given yourself an opportunity to start from your *why*.

Some of the best work and the best relationships I have had with my customers started like that, with my *why*:

"I have a passion for unlocking potential in people and organizations, I'm really good at it, and I would like to help you—I will hold your hand. So, let me start by spending a little time with you and your organization to understand what needs to be done, so you can be a successful leader."

That is a very different approach from "Let me tell you what you should do." That is starting with *what*, and it doesn't inspire.

When working with purpose, your purpose and organizational *why* should reflect an ambition. It should be a *burning ambition* that tells the story of how you serve and how you make the world a better place.

This is opposed to the mainstream way of driving change and performance, talking about a *burning platform*.

A burning platform sparks fear. It's something you want to get away from, it's limiting, and it creates stress. As a leader you can use it to push for action and behavioral change.

But a burning ambition is much more valuable and effective in terms of high performance. It sparks engagement, loyalty, innovation, and teamwork, and is a pull factor. It's something we want to move toward. It's a compelling picture we want to be part of and contribute to.

Your organization might find itself in a situation accurately described as a burning platform. The most effective way to address it is to translate that situation into a burning ambition that resonates with your organizational purpose, or *why*, and talk to the *why* of your employees.

When we communicate our purpose, passion, or cause first, we communicate in a way that drives decision-making and behavior. Sometimes we say that we communicate with the heart.

This way of communicating taps into the part of the brain that influences behavior.[28]

As Sinek says, people don't buy *what* you do, they buy *why* you do it.

And *what* you do simply serves as the tangible proof of what you believe.

From a communication point of view, a good way of looking at this is by transforming Simon Sinek's Golden Circle into a megaphone:

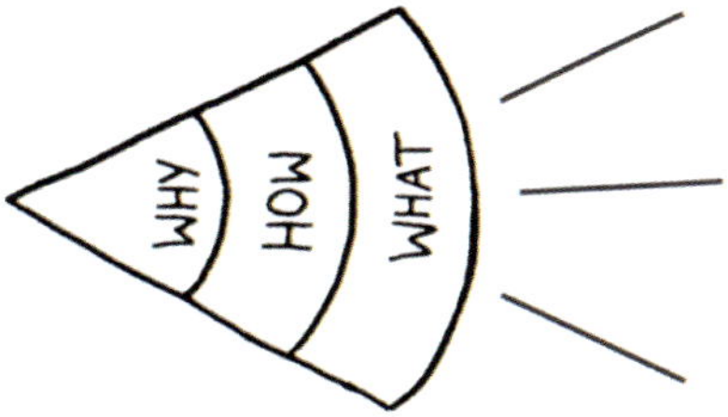

[28] The amygdala, considered part of the limbic system, is shown in research to perform a primary role in the processing of memory, decision-making, and emotional responses.

For a message to spread, it must be loud *and* clear—as though it's being communicated through a megaphone.

Loud is easy; it just drives sales or buys marketing.

Clear is a lot harder.

When we as individuals and organizations are clear about our purpose, or *why*, everyone, from employees to customers, can understand it.

Clarity invites interaction, so people and organizations can choose to work with you, be your champion, and tap into your passion.

This clarity ideally starts at the top of the organization and moves down from there.

Clarity will inspire our employees to create products, services, solutions, and marketing that bring the *why* to life. When everything we say and do echoes our passion and what we believe, we end up with a message that's loud *and* clear.

It should be obvious by now that a loud and clear purpose, or *why*, is vital to our success as leaders and as organizations—a purpose that is heartfelt and bigger and more than profit. Because people don't buy what you do, they buy why you do it.

When looking at the figures and the potential and the return on investment for working with organizational happiness in the context of purpose, strengths, and compassion, I think the case is very compelling for most organizations.

To find your purpose using the Golden Circle and the megaphone, you must have

1. the clarity of why,
2. the discipline of how, and
3. the consistency of what.

Every section of the Golden Circle is equally important. The most important thing is a balance across all three areas, and if you articulate your *why* but your actions and behavior are different, you will fail. So if Coca-Cola wants to sell a story of humanity, it would be a contradiction for that company to use child labor. This is where we see “shit storms” happening—when your actions and behaviors are not aligned with your *why.*

So here is the recipe. Start with the purpose: the *why.*

WHY

If you don’t know why you do what you do, how can you expect anyone else to know? For others to know your *why*, you must first have clarity about your own *why.*

Your organizational purpose and *why* is not something that is developed by your marketing department or brand bureau. It has to be integrated into your organizational culture. It’s a soul-seeking exercise, and it has to be authentic. It can make you cry. You have to mean it.

HOW

Your actions and behavior as a leader and your employees’ actions and behavior bring your mission to life and must be aligned with your passion, values, guiding principles, strengths, and beliefs. This is all about strengths (chapter 5), compassion, leadership, and culture (chapter 6). We will get back to that, but for now this is about making sure the behaviors tell the same story.

WHAT

Everything you say and everything you do must be consistent with what you believe. We live in the tangible world. The only way people will know what you believe will be if you say and do the things you actually believe—if you walk the talk.

This is not just about communication. It also provides some insight into how great organizations are structured.

The *what*, at the end of the megaphone or the outer portion of the Golden Circle, are the things the organization says and does that breathe life into the *why*. They make it tangible.

An organization communicates its *why* through everything it says and does and produces: the marketing, the branding, the products and services. For a company such as Coca-Cola, this can be tricky: They are balancing on a knife's edge when they tell brand stories around humanity while their products are linked to obesity and other lifestyle diseases. It's a constant balance.

As leaders we align our strategy and decision-making with a *why* that responds to the needs of our stakeholders (employees, customers, society) and is grounded in the heart of what we do.

We continue to evaluate where we are in our process and what needs to change—taking concrete steps to make that happen.

Here is what you can do to get from strategy to action:

1. Articulate your purpose and *why.*

   - Define a clear purpose for your organization.
   - Be ambitious and inspiring *and* grounded in the reality of what you can deliver.
   - Convey your purpose in terms of the long-term value created for the people you serve.
   - Communicate success stories to current and future employees and customers.

2. Integrate your purpose and *why.*

   - Develop a simple integration plan and commit to delivering on it. Walk the talk.
   - Focus where it matters most. Think, *What's the one thing that would have the biggest effect?*
   - Use purpose as a lens through which to make decisions.

3. Accelerate the journey.

    - Make sure senior leadership champions purpose and demonstrates their commitment through their words and actions.
    - Establish a feedback culture.
    - Encourage and incentivize middle managers to act in the interest of purpose.
    - Make purpose a day-to-day experience for your employees.
    - Measure and reward decisions and behaviors that align to your organization's purpose.

Make it all stick by measuring, monitoring, and following up. You need to know your Motivational Landscape.

Go, Go!

At this point I encourage you to make a note—mental or by writing it below—about what you are inspired to do around your purpose and *why*.

Think about your organizational purpose and *why*, and your own passion and *why*:

What's the one thing that, if you did it, would have the greatest effect on you and your organization or team?

My one thing on purpose and *why*:

To

So that

Because

CHAPTER 5

STRENGTHS

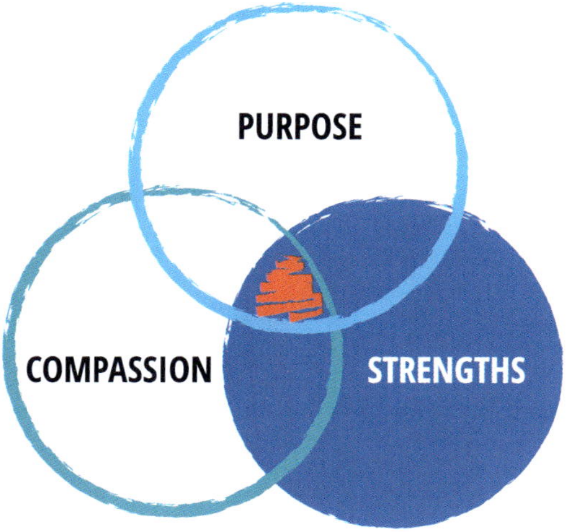

The second pillar of organizational happiness

Strengths-based leadership and real talent management discovers people's talents, strengths, and potential and puts them into play for the purpose of the organization.

Strengths are your superpowers. When you work from a place of strengths and superpowers in the direction of a heartfelt purpose, you feel a sense of engagement, contribution, achievement, and meaning. According to the science of happiness and as we saw from the PERMA model, these are building blocks for happiness and therefore an important pillar of organizational happiness. Your superpowers are also the breeding place of high performance and exceptional results.

A good sign that you are playing to your strengths is when you find yourself in a position that many people see as complex and you have the feeling, *How hard can it be?* Or maybe you are surprised by the praise you get for "just doing" something trivial. Or maybe you are frustrated by other people's inability to see or do something you think can be "done in no time."

This is a good sign that you are using your superpowers. Using them gives you energy, feels easy and natural, and makes you feel good.

This chapter is about strengths and strengths-based leadership.

So, what's the superpower strategy for your organization?

I have done a lot of strengths assessments and participated in more than two thousand feedback sessions related to talent and strengths assessments with the aim of identifying talent, potential, and superpowers. In my opinion, this is at the core of unlocking potential.

Most leaders recognize the competitive advantages that can come with "human capital," "talent management," "well-being," and so on, yet the talent practices their organization subscribe to are stuck in the twentieth century.

We still talk about our employees as our most important resource. We mention *human capital* in our reporting and focus on human resources management. That's exactly what it is: management of resources.

Human resources management is not a winning strategy. It's a mistake to look at the people in an organization as mere resources.

Our organizations are complex organisms with unique individuals with unique talents, potential, and superpowers. You can't unlock the potential by managing resources. You need an integrated superpower strategy—or a real talent management strategy—to catalyze that.

To develop an integrated superpower strategy for your organization, we need to know what we are talking about.

We talk about strengths, talents, and potential in the same sentence yet too often don't pay attention to what we really mean and the context in which we are using that terminology.

What is the difference between a talent and a strength?[29]

Talents are naturally recurring patterns of thought, feeling, or behavior that can be productively applied. [30]

What you know reveals more about your experiences and education than about who you are at the core. Behavior derived from knowledge and skills can be changed far more easily than talent-based behavior.

Talent can't be subordinated. It's constant and enduring. That's what makes it talent. Understanding the difference between the two sources of behavior is essential when you want to develop a superpower strategy as a pillar for organizational happiness.

---

[29] I think Gallup has the clearest and most no-nonsense explanation in this field. See more at www.gallup.com.

[30] According to Gallup's definition.

For example, being drawn to strangers and enjoying the challenge of making a connection with them are talents, whereas the ability to consistently build a network of supporters who know you and are prepared to help you is a strength. To build this strength, you have refined your talents with skills and knowledge. Likewise, the tendency to be perceived as direct or convincing is a talent, whereas the ability to sell successfully is a strength. To persuade others to buy your product, you must combine your talent with product knowledge and certain selling skills.

As leaders responsible for strategies, we talk competently about talent management and employee engagement, but we don't have real strategies—operational strategies and management practices—for playing to our strengths in the direction of our purpose and unlocking the potential in our organizations.

What we as leaders are looking for is this: to lead our people, use our superpowers, and identify and unlock potential. That's *strengths-*

based leadership. And it requires practices, behaviors, and a culture that supports such leadership.

The strengths pillar of the Happiness Sweet Spot offers a framework for implementing strategies on strengths-based leadership.

Think about this: If you—looking at yourself—had to name one superpower, what would it be?

What is it you can do better than others?

If this is difficult for you or you need input for reflection and guidance, I would recommend the CliftonStrengths assessment[31]—formerly StrengthsFinder 2.0—from Gallup, and the VIA Survey[32] on finding your character strengths. Combined, more than twenty-five million people have used these two assessments and tools. (I elaborate more on them later in this chapter.)

---

31 https://www.gallupstrengthscenter.com.

32 http://www.viacharacter.org/www/.

Your strengths are your power.

Your values are what you do with it! They relate to your personal purpose and *why*. Your values are motivators.

Strengths-based leadership and investing in developing employees' talents and strengths is big. It's huge. It represents a fundamental shift in how we as leaders and professionals see and believe in people and organizational development.

It is my experience that if you focus on what works and what is right, this will help you in the most effective way to unlock people's potential and facilitate team performance.

Although almost every leader and organization believes in investing in developing employees' strengths as part of performance management and talent management strategies, different types of leaders take somewhat different approaches.

From an organizational point of view the essence of the strategy is this: Spend time and resources discovering and defining the talents of all employees (everybody has talent), and invest in developing them into strengths. Then put them in into play for your organizational purpose and *why*.

If you do that as a leader, and if all your leader-colleagues are doing that, you are unlocking the potential and catalyzing high performance in your organization.

That is easier said than done. How do you make it happen? How do you get from talking about it and putting it on paper (strategy) to action (behavior)?

Although many experts, thought leaders, authors, and practitioners—myself included—have an opinion about what really works and how best to approach an effective talent management strategy—or, should we say, an effective strengths management strategy—I will mention three sources of great inspiration for me, where you can seek further inspiration, guidance, and hands-on recommendations on working with strengths and strengths-based leadership:

1. Gallup, and Gallup books by Tom Rath (*StrengthsFinder 2.0*) and by Rath and Barry Conchie (*Strengths Based Leadership: Great Leaders, Teams, and Why People Follow*).[33]
2. David Cooperrider[34]
3. Peter Drucker[35]

And of course, Martin Seligman, whom I mentioned earlier in the section on the science of happiness and the PERMA model. In 2004, Christopher Peterson and Martin Seligman came out with *Character Strengths and Virtues: A Handbook and Classification*.[36] This classification

---

[33] www.gallupstrengthscenter.com

[34] Including the book *Strengths-Based Leadership Handbook* by Pernille Hippe Brun, David Cooperrider, and Mikkel Ejsing.

[35] Beginning with his classic book *The Effective Executive* from 1967.

[36] Peterson and Seligman, Character Strengths and Virtues.

is the foundation for the VIA Character Strength test I referred to above and will explore below.

In this chapter I have quoted these experts and thought leaders and authors where appropriate. And I have used their insights to make a simple actionable framework, combining it with my practical experience and superpower to "see" what really works.

The strengths pillar of the Happiness Sweet Spot is all about strengths, strengths-based leadership, and finding, developing, and naming superpowers. You have to know your own superpower and know the superpowers of your team.

This means that you and your team can do what you do best and put your strengths and superpower in play for the purpose of your organization.

Knowing the difference between talent, potential, and strengths is not just important for the HR or talent nerd. It's of essence when you are developing your superpower strategy—or real talent management strategy—and want to focus your organization on strengths-based leadership and creating your organizational happiness strategy.

The key to building a fully developed strength or superpower is to identify your talents and then complement them with acquired knowledge and skills. You have to make an investment in your talent to make it a strength or a superpower.

As a starting point, a strength is developed in the individual, the employee. First, we need to identify the strengths of our employees.

We leaders are looking to build high-performing teams with the strengths we have, but first we must know our teams.

In the short term, we are looking for already developed strengths. But from a longer-term perspective, we are looking for talents and potential to develop into strengths.

That is also true when we are recruiting or trying to attract talent to our organization. We are looking for strengths that fit what we need and for talent and potential we can develop, so that our organization—and business—grows.

To simplify: *Talent* is your natural pattern for thinking, feeling, and doing. It represents your *potential*. You develop your *strengths* and superpowers from your talents.

Talents are the breeding ground for strengths. Underdeveloped talents often end up useless or can even become a source of frustration.

Start with yourself. If you start with identifying your talents and focus on them, you accelerate your learning curve—and get a higher return on investment for your time and energy. It's unlocking your potential in the most effective and fun way.

When you know what you are really good at as a leader, figure out how you can use that knowledge and insight to help your employees find their superpowers.

Of course, we could—as many organizations still do—choose to start identifying weaknesses and try to develop those into strengths. Organizations with this culture—"we fix the weaknesses and overcome problems"—very often have annual appraisal talks or performance reviews that identify weaknesses and make development plans related to them.

This is a losing battle in terms of unlocking the potential in the organization. If you want to use the strengths of the people in your organization as a competitive advantage, you need to focus on talents so you can develop strengths and superpowers.

So, make the natural focus on strengths part of the organizational culture.

When we in the Happiness Sweet Spot model and Motivational Landscape talk about the enormous amount of unlocked potential in organizations, right here is an important key: Focus your investments on developing talents into superpowers. That's about releasing the individual, setting them free, and unlocking potential.

It's a win-win situation. The organization will more likely experience sustainable success, and the employees will have a sense of achievement, meaning, and engagement, which are building blocks for happiness: happy employees and organizational happiness.

Strengths Assessments and Tests

As mentioned in the beginning of this chapter, a quick and efficient way to start discovering and identifying talents and strengths is by using a strengths or talent assessment.

Start by knowing who you are as a leader and get to know your superpowers. You need them to unlock the potential of your employees and organization. I will get back to that, but first I will give you a few tips on how to identify superpowers.

Again, I recommend and use the CliftonStrengths assessment, formerly StrengthsFinder, from Gallup, and the VIA Survey on character strengths.

Two of the most recent and important thought leaders on strengths and strengths-based leadership are Marcus Buckingham and Donald O. Clifton. Buckingham was coauthor of the national best seller *First, Break All the Rules,* and Clifton was chairman of the Gallup International Research and Education Center.

In 2001 they published the book *Now, Discover Your Strengths.* At the heart of the book is the StrengthsFinder Profile. Gallup has conducted psychological profiles of more than two million people to develop the assessment.

It is a widely accepted approach to discovering what you naturally do best and learning more about how to develop your talents.[37]

The other well-researched and widely accepted and used strengths assessment I would recommend looking at is the VIA Survey, which is free and can be taken online.

The VIA Survey[38] is a psychometrically validated personality test that measures an individual's character strengths. Character strengths in this context are viewed as our

---

37 https://www.gallupstrengthscenter.com/.

38 https://www.viacharacter.org/www/Character-Strengths-Survey.

positive personality in the way that they are our core capacities for thinking, feeling, and behaving in ways that can bring benefit to us and to others.

In 2001, the VIA Institute on Character was established as a nonprofit organization to advance the science and practice of character and to fill the world with greater virtue (more wisdom, courage, humanity, justice, temperance, and transcendence). Through the support of the Myerson Foundation and the leadership of Dr. Martin Seligman and Dr. Chris Peterson, the VIA Classification of Character Strengths, as well as the publication *Character Strengths and Virtues* (VIA's handbook), were written. Upon its publication it was hailed as the "backbone of positive psychology."

The VIA Survey was designed specifically to measure twenty-four character strengths. Since its inception, the VIA Survey has been, and still is, offered for free by the VIA Institute so that "every individual in the world can 'know their 24' and use this information to lead happier, thriving lives."

I have used many tools, assessments, and tests to facilitate and catalyze conversations about employees' talents, potential, and strengths.

These kinds of tools should not be complicated, and people shouldn't think they will provide "the answer." This should not be a religion, but a helpful tool.

Be careful not to fall into the trap of "talent assessments" that are poorly researched, not validated, and play the talent management game in a complex way. If you introduce complex models and practices around this, you are not getting to the "action" part. You will be sucked up in the "strategy" part. And your strategy will be only words on paper.

The market and business model for licensing of tests attracts "gold diggers" with no intention of helping you and no ability to do so.

I think CliftonStrengths and the VIA Survey do the job in a simple no-nonsense way that is easy to understand.

Ideally you would want to use these tools on your whole team and in your whole organization, so you can complement superpowers and build high-performing teams.

You might need a little guidance or have your managers get a little training to kick it off, but you don't need a full-time organizational psychologist or senior management consultant to understand the assessments and implement your strategy on strengths-based leadership.

Strengths-Based Leadership

Some leaders see their role as managing resources in the best possible way.

That's not a winning strategy.

Strengths-based leadership is a field with many experts and many brilliant thinkers. So, to cut a very long story short, I will quote the late Peter Drucker, a management guru who first paid real attention to strengths-based management and leadership in his book *The Effective Executive* (1967):

> *"The task of leadership is to create an alignment of strengths in ways that make weaknesses irrelevant."*

The best leaders know and value the unique abilities and even the crazy superpowers of their employees, and they know how or learn how to put them into play for the purpose of the team and organization. The best leaders are strengths-based leaders.

When I advise leaders and organizations on strengths-based leadership or do leadership training, I often say that you and everybody on your team need to know four things:

1. What am I really good at? (superpower)
2. What's my job? (purpose and goal setting)
3. How am I doing? (feedback)
4. What can I do to develop? (development plan)

Number five would be for you as a leader to know how to activate the strengths of the people on your team.

That's it! That's strengths-based leadership.

I just gave you a few tips on finding your superpowers, but before you can lead effectively and authentically, you need to consider how you want to be as a leader. What style fits your personality and superpowers well?

There are many ways of describing management styles, and many books have been written about the "right" leadership style.

We often look to role models and mirror people we see playing their role as leader in a way we like and that seems to make them successful.

Of course, we can adapt to a role that we have learned to play.[39] Or we can try to mirror someone else who has an effective leadership style.

But the truth is that we can't all be Richard Branson, Nelson Mandela, Mother Teresa, or Jack Welch. And if we learn to play a role that is not authentic, our employees feel it.

It's ineffective to be unauthentic.

We all know the feeling of seeing a speaker who functionally has learned "effective body language," but whose presentation nonetheless feels fake. Or the feeling of the "effective handshake."

---

[39] Frameworks like Situational Leadership subscribe to that approach.

If you are fake, you can't lead effectively, so find and develop a leadership style that fits your personality and your superpowers.

We might aspire to be a great leader, but to be a great leader you need to be authentic.

As Oscar Wilde supposedly said, "Be yourself. Everyone else is already taken."

Authentic leadership is about being yourself, knowing yourself—and knowing your superpowers, so they can be a part of your way of leading.

Discovering your authentic leadership style is about

1. learning from your life story,
2. knowing the authentic you (your superpowers),
3. practicing your values—what you do with your superpowers,
4. practicing your governing principles,
5. balancing internal and external motivations, and

6. having a support team.[40]

And how do you know? Great results over a sustained period of time is the ultimate mark of an authentic leader—a leader who is aware of being authentic and has an eye for the dynamics of organizational happiness.

This section was about you as the leader, finding your superpowers and using them for the purpose of the organization.

Why is focusing on strengths and superpowers going to make you successful?

---

40 George, Sims, McLean, and Mayer, "Discovering Your Authentic Leadership."

Why Strengths?

Because playing to strengths and developing talents is unlocking your organizational potential—and it's a big part of the competitive advantage we talk about when we work seriously with organizational happiness and the Happiness Sweet Spot.

Gallup published a study in 2015 showing that employee engagement was a function of how much leaders in the organization focused on each employee's strengths and developing their talents.

If you focus on strengths and what's working well, you will have high employee engagement.

Gallup conducted research and surveyed almost 200,000 employees based on twelve questions around employee engagement—now known as Gallup's Q12 engagement survey.[41]

[41] See Gallup.com for more research and guidance.

The statement found to have the biggest correlation to and effect on productivity was this one:

"At work I have the opportunity to do what I do best every day."

In your Motivational Landscape[42] we ask people to respond to this statement: "I have the opportunity to do what I do best."

As demonstrated by the research and many other good examples, there is a direct correlation between people's ability to use their strengths at work and their productivity as well as their organization's productivity.

Employees who "strongly agree" with that one statement also tend to be part of a high-performing team with low turnover, higher retention rates, and higher customer satisfaction.

---

[42] See www.MotivationalLandscape.com.

You could consider asking your employees just that one question every week to get data on your engagement.

At Motivational Landscape we played with the thought. But organizational happiness and developing a true competitive advantage for your organization is more than being able to use your strengths at work every day and being wrapped up in strengths-based leadership.

Development of your talents and potential and use of your strengths for the purpose of the organization generates a feeling of fulfillment. And having a sense of engagement, achievement, and purpose is an important building block for happiness[43] and conducive to organizational happiness and finding the Happiness Sweet Spot for your organization.

Your strengths quest both as an organization and as a person is a strategy and an adventure.

---

[43] The PERMA model as referred to in chapter 1

Playing to your strengths leads to happiness.

And it's good for business too.

So, what's not to like?

It should be obvious by now that strengths-based leadership and finding and developing your superpowers is a powerful advantage in being successful in what you do as an organization.

The business case is compelling. It sounds compelling. It's an easy, positive sell.

How is playing to strengths and developing talents done in real—organizational—life?

How To

Suppose I asked you these five questions:

1. "What was the best day you've had at work in the last six months?"
2. "What were you doing that day?"
3. "Why did you enjoy it?"
4. "What do you need from me as your leader to be in that spot more often?"
5. "When can I count on you?"

We would have started a conversation about talent, potential, using your strengths—and strengths-based leadership.

Playing to your strengths and choosing strengths-based leadership has a lot to do with the conversations you have in your organization.

We use different terms: *conversations, questions coaching, feedback, meetings, teamwork.* It's really about the fact that we prioritize discovering and having conversations about what makes each person unique. What are your superpowers? What are mine? And how can I serve you or help you develop and use your superpowers for our purpose?

That makes a real difference in terms of results and creating an effective, high-performing, and happy organization.

Our strengths aren't always on display. Sometimes they require precise triggering to turn on. If you do it right, you will see real engagement, motivation, and high performance. If you do it wrong, you will lock that person down.

Your job as a strengths-based leader is also to add and facilitate what doesn't come naturally in the current situation. Help your employees discover how to replace a weakness with a strength.

One employee requires regular appraisal; another one requires independence. For yet another, performance is related to the time of day she works best and is most alert.

The most powerful trigger by far is recognition, not money.

We have to appreciate and accept that we all have different personalities, motivations, and triggers: how we think, how patient we are, how we build relationships, how secure we need to feel, what challenges us, what drives us, and what our goals are.

We all thrive and perform differently under different circumstances, depending on the leadership style, team, culture, and values. That is why some people are star performers and thrive tremendously in one organization, yet fail to perform when they are headhunted to their competitor. The subject of "portable talent" and applying the right leadership style is an interesting one.[44]

---

[44] See more on "portable talent" in *Chasing Stars* by Boris Groysberg and "Learn How to Spot Portable Talent," by Claudio Fernández-Aráoz.

These differences in traits and talents have been described as similar to blood types: They cut across the superficial variations of race, sex, and age and capture the essential uniqueness of each individual.

For us as leaders, it is essential that we bring this reality and insight to our actions and interactions when we connect, build teams, and catalyze high performance.

You need to constantly adjust and catalyze your team and organization so that the unique contributions, the unique needs, and the unique style of each employee can be given free rein. Release and unlock the potential. Your success as a leader will depend almost entirely on your ability to do this in your authentic, genuine way of leading. A leader's success is based solely on the success of their followers.

Great leadership is about releasing and unlocking potential. It's not about transformation.

Releasing and unlocking potential is all about playing to your organizational strengths—the strengths of your employees and high-performing teams, which ultimately generate sustainable results.

From an organizational and strategic point of view it is fair to say that in the short term, taking immediate action means identifying strengths and making sure your organization provides a frame, an environment, and a (leadership) culture that puts these strengths into play for your mission: your purpose.

In the long term, you need to create a superpower strategy: How will you identify, develop, and invest in your employees' talents so they become strengths and superpowers that are useful for the organization and unlock potential?

This is also about providing strengths-based feedback and coaching. Asking questions like the five I listed earlier will give you a place to start.

Strengths-based leaders know their own superpowers and the superpowers of their team members. They know how to use the superpowers of their team. They know which person is the right one for each job. And they know how team members complement each other and how each person helps the performance of the team.

When we're part of a high-performing team, we know our own strengths as well as the strengths of our team members. And we know how to trigger them and bring them into play, because we have a structure to talk about it so we can create stronger, more productive teams.

You can make offer your managers a coach or train them in coaching skills. A coach can help them reflect on practices, set goals, and work toward strengths, and be an objective sounding board who can articulate the things that need to be worked on.

We can find the value of bringing compassion to our leadership, something we'll talk about more in the next chapter. It can help us identify our employees' real strengths by seeking to better understand and know those we lead—what motivates them to aim for better and to learn, grow, and develop.

By bringing compassion to work and increasing our awareness of where our employees thrive through the work they do and how they become high performers, we can better identify opportunities to help them feel like what they do matters (brings meaning) and become stronger contributors to our organization and purpose.

Go, Go!

At this point I encourage you to make a note—mental or by writing it below—about what you are inspired to do around strengths and strengths-based leadership.

Think about strengths and strengths-based leadership:

What's the one thing that, if you did it, would have the greatest effect on you and your organization or team?

My one thing on strengths and strength-based leadership:

To

So that

Because

CHAPTER 6

COMPASSION

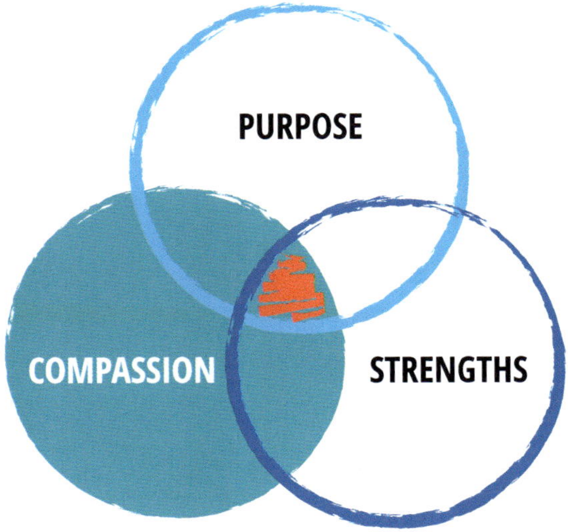

The third pillar of organizational happiness

What does it mean to cultivate a culture of compassion? Compassion is essential to leadership. It means being interested in understanding the difficulties of other people and having a burning desire to help them.

Compassion is defined by your leadership and culture. That's it! Compassion is a crucial part of your organizational culture. It's about "the way we do things around here" and how we treat each other.

I believe that the key to a happier and more successful society is the cultivation and growth of compassion at every level—individual, organizational, and national.

In this chapter I look at compassion as part of culture and as a leadership discipline or style. I explore what compassion is, what it looks like in organizations, and why cultivating a culture of compassion is good for business, contributing to its performance and success.

At the end of the chapter is a "recipe" that on a more practical level gives you guidance and help with how to get from strategy to action—and make it stick.

We often hear that culture is your competitive advantage. I think it's too easy talk about culture like that, because how do you define culture?

Organizational culture is more nuanced than simply defining culture as culture. Culture needs to be "unwrapped."

Culture is about your people, your habits, and your purpose.

And if you are able to cultivate a culture of compassion, you have taken a grand step toward your Organizational Happiness Sweet Spot.

The word *compassion* does not always come to mind when we talk about leadership, competitive advantage, business models, and creating a high-performing organization.

But it should.

I think there is or will be a trend toward cultivating compassion in organizations and in our societies as we look for something "more," something more "right" and more genuine, where we serve and take care of each other and our employees. That is compassion.

There is a connection to and an overlap with what we call "servant leadership."[45] Servant leadership is a leadership philosophy in which the main goal of the leader is to serve. A servant leader shares power, puts the needs of the employees first, and helps people develop and perform as highly as possible.[46]

This is also a form of compassion. And compassionate leadership is more than that. Compassionate leadership will be big, as part of a leadership style and as a building block for

---

[45] The term *servant leadership* was coined by Robert K. Greenleaf in "The Servant as Leader," an essay first published in 1970.

[46] Autry, The Servant Leader.

unlocking potential and creating a unique competitive advantage.

As mentioned earlier, research[47] has demonstrated that leaders who project warmth are more effective than those who exude toughness, even before credibility and competence are taken into account. Kindness and warmth evoke trust, which is a building block of performance and teamwork.

This is important. As leaders we should know what good leadership looks like and what bad leadership looks like in our organization. We should recognize good leadership behavior and know what behavior is not acceptable.

Researchers at Oxford University analyzed hundreds of published papers that studied the relationship between kindness and happiness. They uncovered twenty-one studies that explicitly prove that being kind to others makes

---

[47] See the work of Amy Cuddy and her research partners at Harvard Business School.

us happier. Added to that is research from the University of Warwick that revealed that happy people are 12 percent more productive at work than unhappy people.[48]

"Love and compassion at work? Really?"

That's a question I hear often.

Sometimes it's followed by something like, "This happiness crap is one thing...and now you want us to have love and compassion at work too? I'm not sure our board would think it's a good idea or something we should invest in."

I think that attitude or train of thought is a sign of mediocre leadership and a mistake. It's playing it safe. When we look at our organization and our employees as "resources" that need to be managed—i.e., human resource management—we are being mediocre and getting mediocre results.

---

[48] See chapter 2, "The Business Case."

Leadership is also about courage. Dare to lead, put yourself and your heart into it, and set an example for how we treat each other: with love and compassion—even at work.

Be that exceptional leader and create exceptional results.

I will show you why cultivating a culture of compassion is a good idea for you and your organization or business.

Compassion is a basic human emotion that has been largely neglected in terms of organizational development and leadership behavior.

Some organizations try to regulate behavior with standard operating procedures and so on. We have had some extraordinary examples of regulations in organizations that try to limit love and compassion at work.

As a leader I think you have to be very careful and have a very light touch when it comes to regulating levels of love and compassion at work.

Some companies and organizations know firsthand that love and compassion have a place at work and have a strong influence on workplace outcomes.[49] The more love our employees feel at work, the more engaged they are and the happier they are.

In organizations and at work, what we want is "companionate love," which is far less intense than romantic love. Compassion is based on warmth, affection, and connection rather than on passion.

As we define it in the Happiness Sweet Spot, compassion is "an interest in understanding the difficulties of other people *and* a burning desire to help them."

---

[49] Barsade and O'Neill, "Employees Who Feel Love Perform Better."

I think that captures leadership at its best.

Some leaders are afraid of being too personal and too closely connected with others at work, because they think their behavior can or will be misunderstood.

I understand that concern. But cultivating a culture of compassion is possible only if you feel warmth, affection, and connection—at work.

And you need to combine that culture and leadership style with a solid moral compass and strong personal values. As described earlier, your strengths are your superpowers. Your values act as the compass you use to decide what to do with those superpowers.

A culture of compassion is evident "when colleagues who are together day in and day out, ask and care about each other's work and even non-work issues," Sigal Barsade says. "They are careful of each other's feelings. They show compassion when things don't go well. And they also show affection and caring—and that can be about bringing somebody a cup of coffee when you go get your own, or just listening when a co-worker needs to talk."

When I am a keynote speaker and conducting workshops on "how to cultivate a culture of compassion,"[50] my experience is that in some cultures and countries, compassion is easily understood and its value is instantly accepted. It's the most natural thing—part of people's upbringing and teaching.

In some countries and cultures, however, compassion is not accepted or understood. I find this mostly in northern Europe and parts of the United States.

One of the reasons for this difference in embracing the idea of incorporating compassion into organizations is that compassion is often connected to or linked with spirituality.

---

[50] I have experience speaking about compassion in Pakistan, South Africa, the Nordic countries, Europe, Latin America, Asia, and the United States.

Although many of us consider ourselves spiritual human beings, I don't want this chapter to sound overly "spiritual" and alienate the organizations that need the message the most. That's the risk if we use traditional spiritual language that few people can relate to in an organizational context.

So, my message is this: Dive into compassion if it sparks something in you. Or just see compassion as leadership in its essence—an authentic, genuine, and real kind of leadership.

Compassion is leadership and leadership is compassion!

The challenge for leaders is no longer to find a good reason that compassion is good for business. The challenge now is to design work and workplaces that awaken compassion and facilitate compassionate leadership in the best way.

For this chapter I would like to mention three sources of great inspiration. This is also where you can seek further guidance and hands-on recommendations for cultivating a culture of compassion:

1. The Dalai Lama[51]
2. Monica Worline and Jane Dutton, *Awakening Compassion at Work*[52]
3. Sigal Barsade and Olivia A. O'Neill's research study "What's Love Got to Do with It?"[53]

In this chapter I have quoted these experts and thought leaders and authors where appropriate.

---

[51] One of the sources from the Dalai Lama on this subject is "Compassion as the Source of Happiness," which can be found at www.DalaiLama.com.

[52] Full publication information is in the bibliography.

[53] Full publication information is in the bibliography.

Compassion, Terrorism, and Peace Building in South Asia

Over a period of ten years I was engaged as an expert and advisor in a troubled region in Asia related to leadership, capacity building, counterterrorism missions, and peace building.

I worked closely with police and prosecutors on counterterrorism initiatives to enhance cooperation so that terrorists could be prosecuted more effectively.

It is of course an intense environment—very macho and conflict/fight oriented. You need to have a strong *why* and personal purpose to flourish in that setting.

In the beginning of the missions we all focused on professional competencies like human resource management, key performance indicators, leadership, project management, and so on. We only really scratched the surface when we delivered the reports and documented capacity building and results.

I found it difficult to facilitate the cooperation and teamwork. We were tackling conflict and peace building without a sense of trust and connection—without compassion.

This changed over the years as I worked on these projects. We were able to build trust so that conflicts became opportunities to grow and connect.

That didn't happen by itself.

One of the simple things I did was set up informal meetings and dinners with small groups of people (five to eight) with the theme "My Dream." Just that. At those "dream meetings" we shared personal stories about our lives, families, and dreams for a better future. We followed three guidelines: (1) Be present as you listen to other people's dreams, (2) don't try to "fix" other people's dreams, and (3) know you can offer to help.

I deliberately went first at these "dream meetings" and put all my heart into these conversations. I emphasized love and compassionate leadership: understanding the difficulties of others and having a burning desire to help them.

My observation and experience were that this completely changed the environment and "culture" around the important stuff we wanted to succeed with. There was less fighting, and people were more inclined to set aside their personal agendas. And there was more compassion and cooperation.

We were a lot more effective and successful with our mission when there was love and compassion among us.

We unlocked the potential.

I was given the nickname "the Gentle Giant from Denmark," something for which I was very grateful. Later, when they asked me to come and help on missions, some of the guys said, "We need the Gentle Giant here to help us out."

When we treat ourselves and others compassionately, we tend to come together in a contributory manner that raises the group to greater heights as a whole. With this, bonds are formed, trust is established, and a willingness to work together on projects and have a shared vision becomes the driving force behind our intentions.

Why Compassion

Compassion increases employee loyalty, and trust boosts individual and team performance by being conducive to feeling "safe." Compassion facilitates the spirit of experimentation and is critical for creativity and innovation.

According to research,[54] employees who felt they worked in a loving, caring culture reported higher levels of satisfaction and teamwork. They showed up to work more often.

Approximately one in five adults in the United States—43.8 million, or 18.5 percent—experience mental illness and/or depression in a given year. This is a relatively high rate. The main cause of depression is not a lack of material necessities but being deprived of the affection of others.[55]

---

54 Barsade and O'Neill, "Employees Who Feel Love Perform Better."

55 National Institute of Mental Health. "Prevalence of Any Mental Illness."

In terms of establishing, creating, and cultivating a strong culture, my advice is to be careful that you're not too rigid about processes and formalized operating procedures. I recommend a very light touch in this respect.

It can be tempting to create a box where everybody needs to fit in to be part of the organization. I call this "the fit-in model." It's tempting because then we can create processes and guidelines around it. We can even measure cultural fit.

But that is not leadership. That's called managing resources. It does not release and unlock potential.

If you as a leader want high performance—plus organizational happiness and high employee engagement—you will have to take the sometimes-difficult role of creating an environment where there is room for the crazy, unique superpowers so that you can use them for your mission and strategy. And sometimes you have to build a team around those superpowers, because those superpowers are needed to do something new or extraordinary. Sometimes those superpowers need to be cultivated and supported.

Creating or cultivating a culture of compassion in your organization is where many companies are focusing their attention.

Whole Foods Market has a set of management principles that begin with "Love." PepsiCo lists "caring" as its first guiding principle on its website. Zappos also explicitly focuses on caring as part of its values: "We are more than a team though—we are a family. We watch out for each other, care for each other, and go above and beyond for each other."

When people come together in a supportive environment and feel safe from competition, there is less fear. There is less fear of failure, which results in better creativity, innovation, and performance. The feeling of being psychologically safe enhances performance.[56]

When we cultivate a culture of compassion, we facilitate an environment and a leadership culture where "I trust that it's OK to make mistakes."

The more we care for the well-being and happiness of others, the greater our own sense of well-being becomes.

Cultivating a culture of compassion such as a close, warm-hearted feeling for others automatically puts the mind at ease. This helps remove whatever fears or insecurities we may have and gives us the strength to cope with our challenges.

As the Dalai Lama says about compassion, "It is the ultimate source of success in life."

---

[56] Duhigg, "What Google Learned From Its Quest to Build the Perfect Team."

We can strive gradually to become more compassionate—that is, we can develop both genuine interest in and sympathy toward our employees' difficulties and the will to help them. As a result, we as leaders feel better and stronger.

To be the best in your leadership role, it's important for you to develop compassion toward yourself. I meet many leaders who constantly say, "I could do better" and "I could do more." This comes from a feeling of "not enough." It's a limiting belief that kills your energy.

If you practice self-compassion as a leader, you feel like you're "enough" and come across much more clearly, with strong energy. You can communicate from an authentic place that inspires people to action.

It is obvious by now that cultivating compassion and developing compassionate leadership is a powerful advantage in being successful in what you do as an organization.

Next I'll share advice on how to cultivate a culture of compassion.

How to Cultivate a Culture of Compassion

Cultivating a culture of compassion is simple, yet human emotions and organizational behavior and development always come with complexity. No two organizations and no two leaders are the same.

Your organization is a unique organism, and your employees are unique human beings with their own motivations.

One size does not fit all. And leadership means choosing to dive into the complexity and diversity without having all the answers. But you can bravely cultivate a culture that is conducive to sustainable success.

You can cultivate a culture of compassion.

It takes courage and heart to lead. It means practicing your values, choosing courage over comfort, and daring to lead.[57]

Compassion is shown in the small moments between employees—a warm smile, a kind note, a sympathetic ear—day after day, month after month, helping to create and maintain a strong culture of compassion and leading to employee engagement, productivity, and customer satisfaction.

Support, practice, and facilitate that as a leader.

On the other hand, organizational messages that endorse winning at all costs or prioritizing self-promotion undermine compassion in your organization.

---

[57] Brené Brown has done inspiring research and framed leadership in her book *Dare to Lead: Brave Work. Tough Conversations. Whole Hearts.*

Your organizational storytelling, brand, and message are very important when you develop organizational happiness and cultivate a culture of compassion.

What messages do we send when we use phrases such as "we want to win market share," "we are warriors," "the war for talent," "rearm our team," and other highly competitive and battle-related references? A message of competition, war, and fear. That's not conducive to compassion. It undermines compassion.

As compassionate leaders we should be telling stories about our organization's purpose and *why*. We should inspire employees by talking about our organization's accomplishments, emphasizing its desire to make the world better and our commitment to doing good.

The capacity to deeply relate to others is key to all forms of relational success—at work and at home. If you are a leader, notice this: Leaders who give the least amount of positive guidance to their subordinates are less successful in achieving their organizations' goals, and their employees are unhappier with their work.

By not taking an active role in dialogue and team building, you generate more interpersonal conflicts within groups.

You could try having leaders model their own vulnerability—or do it yourself—to help create an atmosphere of safety and trust.

It could be as simple as saying, "I don't know" or "I need help."

Research suggests that compassion isn't something you're necessarily born with. Instead, it can be developed through practice.

Most of the decisions we make on any given day are not derived from a rational mind-set but from a response to our emotionally driven network of mirror neurons, where we seek commonality with those around us and connection to the work we do.

And that means that compassionate leadership includes a genuine, honest, and humble approach that allows us to tap into the superpowers, strengths, creativity, and insights of our employees.

To effectively lead others, we need to show our employees that we are present to hear, understand, and provide what they require to succeed and thrive under our compassionate leadership.

16 Things You Can Do

Here are sixteen things you can do to cultivate an organizational culture of compassion and develop your compassionate leadership skills:

Pay attention. Look for clues that might suggest someone is suffering—body language, tone of voice, or unusual work patterns—and ask gently in a private setting what might be going on.

Practice presence.[58] In my opinion, this is by far the most important of all leadership skills. If you are able to be here, now, and listen and serve, you can move people and organizations. We are easily distracted and are surrounded with tools and electronics that make being present hard. And even though presence and compassion are what people need, there becomes less of it. Be

---

[58] If you are interested in this, a good recent publication is Aware: The Science and Practice of Presence—A Complete Guide to the Groundbreaking Wheel of Awareness Meditation Practice, by Daniel J. Siegel.

that present leader. Don't hide in emails, diagrams, and KPIs. Say good morning, go for lunch, and practice listening and serving.

Be available. Create opportunities for connection. Keep your door open, stay a little while after meetings, put away your phone, walk and talk, be curious and empathic.

Take compassionate action. Make employees feel safe. Send them a short note. Ask, "How's life?" and be present and show that you want to hear the answer. Offer work flexibility that suits people's family situations. Again, be present, empathic, and available.

Think about the emotions you're expressing to employees every day. Your mood creates a cultural blueprint for the group.

Look at your policies and management practices. Are they conducive to compassion? Do you talk about compassion?

Encourage cooperation, not competition, even through subtle cues.

See people as individuals, not as a number or resource. Look at how you do and present reporting. Acknowledge employees' strengths and positive attributes in front of others.

Don't play the blame game. When we blame others for their misfortune, we feel less tenderness and concern toward them.

Notice and savor how good it feels to be compassionate. As a leader you feel better and stronger when you practice compassion.

Don't be a sponge. When we completely take on other people's suffering as our own, we risk feeling personally distressed, threatened, and overwhelmed; in some cases, this can even lead to burnout. Instead, try to be receptive to other people's feelings without adopting those feelings as your own.

Create a team-working environment. Encourage brainstorms and mastermind meetings. Invite the team to share in the organization's vision and goals, and help create action steps to achieve them. An environment where you can collaborate by sharing ideas and offering creative solutions is one that thrives.

See your employees beyond the roles they play in your organization. Don't treat your employees as a "human resource" or "human capital" or cogs in the organizational wheel, but as full participants in your shared purpose.

Inspire daily acts of kindness. Hold a brainstorming session or challenge teams to come up with daily acts of kindness. When these acts come from the heart and are authentic, they will help spark and fuel a culture of compassion.

Organize team-building activities. This is an opportunity to feel included and connect. Take the lead or ask for a volunteer to set up team-building activities for employees. It can be anything from going mini-golfing to organizing a community cleanup or volunteering with an organization to reduce food waste. Ask your employees to brainstorm ideas and suggestions.

Admit that you don't know everything. It's impossible for anyone to truly know or understand the complexities of what our organization has to address or overcome. If we walk around thinking we are the only ones with enough experience and knowledge to know what needs to be done, how can we truly listen to and understand what our employees face, not to mention what it's really like to work for us?

Go, Go!

At this point I encourage you to make a note—mental or by writing it below—about what you are inspired to do to cultivate a culture of compassion and develop compassionate leadership.

Think about cultivating a culture of compassion in your organization:

What's the one thing that, if you did it, would have the greatest effect on you and your organization or team?

My one thing on compassion:

To

So that

Because

CHAPTER 7

MOTIVATIONAL LANDSCAPE

MOTIVATIONAL LANDSCAPE

We help you get a handle on employee engagement

The Motivational Landscape consists of data on our organizational happiness and employee engagement as if our business depends on it.

Motivational Landscape gives us the data that allow us to manage and lead our people. Because we can and will lead. We dare to lead.

We want to see smoke before it becomes a fire. And we want to share best practices and learn from the best in the organization.

We developed Motivational Landscape because we identified a need to make better people decisions instead of relying on gut feelings when it came to developing strategies for organizational happiness and employee engagement.

Based on interviews with leaders and professionals and our work with the Happiness Sweet Spot implementation, we came up with a simple platform that tells us how we are doing and allows us to measure, monitor, and follow up—as if our people matter as much as our financial performance and our customer satisfaction.

The storytelling on the Motivational Landscape purpose can be captured in the following.

Think about it: You probably have three main key performance indicators, or KPIs, in your organization.

1. financial performance
2. customer satisfaction
3. employee engagement

That's it!

I think it makes a lot of sense if you are able to—and dare to—take some of the complexity out of your strategy, scorecards, and communication and use only those three KPIs.

And instead of using the term *employee engagement*, I think we should start naming it what it really is: *organizational happiness*.

Although most organizations have systems and tools in place to measure, evaluate, and follow up on financial performance and customer satisfaction, it's not the same as having a clear and up-to-date picture of your organizational happiness and employee engagement.

The annual employee engagement survey or staff satisfaction survey does not do that for you. Those processes and reports produce a snapshot of the situation in your organization. And by the time you have that snapshot, it's typically three months old.

Would we accept old data on financial performance?

No, we wouldn't—and we don't.

We have systems and tools in place to report almost in real time how we are doing on financial performance. So why do we accept old data delivered once a year on organizational happiness and employee engagement, when we know it is—or should be—one of our top three strategies for success?

It beats me. When I talk to my organizations about this dilemma, what I hear is excuses for not investing in measuring organizational happiness and employee engagement, and a need for guidance so that "we don't create another heavy HR-process monster that demands a lot of attention and resources from the organization."

What if this were the point of departure for this conversation in the management team:

1. Organizational happiness and employee engagement is a *top priority*—and strategy—for us. Because it makes sense on all levels, including a business one.
2. To take organizational happiness and employee engagement seriously, we want to—and need to—*measure, monitor, and follow up* on it on a regular basis.

3. We want to *see smoke before it becomes a fire* in our organization, and we want to know where in our organization we can learn from the best.
4. How hard can it be? Let's ask our employees ten intelligent questions based on the science of organizational happiness and employee engagement on a regular basis. And let's have the data so we can decide how to manage and lead our people and organization in the best way.

I think there is a simple, operational strategy for organizational happiness and employee engagement right there.

What's Your Motivational Landscape?

It is difficult to focus your efforts and develop a strategy for organizational happiness if you don't know how you are doing.

Do you have clear picture of the employee engagement, motivation, and happiness in your organization?

Do you have a clear, up-to-date picture of the Motivational Landscape across your organization?

If not, how do you find out? And how do you set up a simple feedback system that gives you the data you need in an effective way, without burdening your employees?

I think you should ask your employees once a week or at least once a month.

Use your own survey system, look at the pulse surveys in the market, or take advantage of the work we have done for our clients in this area.[59]

The market for pulse surveys is relatively new.[60] In the beginning I saw many offerings that were driven by "tech nerds" and not so much by "people and leadership nerds." In my view this has led to solutions for employee engagement surveys that are over-engineered. The market is starting to mature in the sense that service providers in this area are starting to provide simple, no-nonsense solutions to having data on employee engagement. Because that is what most organizations need to drive engagement and make the right people decisions.

If you explore the market for pulse surveys, my advice would be to look out for unnecessary complexity and difficult-to-understand algorithms and make sure that questions and

---

59 See www.MotivationalLandscape.com.

60 Bersin, "A New Market Is Born."

surveys are based on science and backed by professionals.

The system and service we have developed started with a fire in Asia.

The Fire in Asia

I work for a small global organization with headquarters in Copenhagen that advises and consults on environmental and climate solutions around the world. About a thousand employees work in this knowledge-heavy environment.

I was called in urgently for a crisis meeting late on a Friday at the end of the month. The subject of the meeting was "Asia: Organizational Damage." With that subject line, I was curious to hear what was going on in Asia.

It turned out that all the employees except the newly recruited managing director for Asia—fifteen people in all—had left to work for a competitor that was building a new Asia organization based in Singapore.

For my client that meant we would have no real presence in Asia. Our Asia strategy was a central part of being a global player in the market, and now it was back to square one. It would take years to rebuild.

The meeting started with a long legal evaluation of employees' competition clauses and protection of intellectual property rights.

At one point the CEO asked, "But why? Why did our valued employees leave us? We praise ourselves for being a first-choice employer in the industry, and we have good rankings in Best Places to Work every year."

The second question was "Why didn't we see it coming? If I had known, I would have taken action."

In a conversation afterward, one of our former key employees in Singapore told me, "The new MD in Singapore is an asshole who practices management by fear. The leadership style is that of the mushroom technique: Keep them in the dark, feed them shit, and when they stick their head out, chop it off."

This was an organization where we had worked on organizational happiness, strengths-based leadership—the whole package. I had personally trained all the managers less than a year earlier. It was time to do our follow-up training and revisit the strategy.

Apparently, this was a recruitment error that had resulted in a catastrophe in a very short time. And we, the experts and advisors, and the CEO were too far away to smell the smoke or see the fire.

Frankly, I was surprised and a bit embarrassed. The CEO asked me in a frustrated tone, "Why didn't we know?"

I said, "Apparently, we didn't have a genuine up-to-date picture of the Motivational Landscape."

We decided that it was crucial, going forward, to measure, monitor, and follow up on organizational happiness and employee engagement every second week, in a simple and operational way.

We devised ten questions to all employees. It takes ninety seconds to respond to them. And we have the data immediately on a dashboard.

So now, just like we have weekly, almost real-time data on financial performance, we have that information on employee engagement too. Our business depends on it!

We want to see smoke before it becomes a fire. (This is a good example of a fire.)

And we want to share best practices and learn from the best in the organization.

We decided that the Motivational Landscape reporting and figures should be part of the standard agenda of every management meeting and every team meeting, just like the financial performance is.

After the Motivational Landscape was implemented in the organization above, we identified one department that consistently had a high score across all three pillars of the Happiness Sweet Spot.

The leader of that department had her own "recipe for success" rooted in her experience, strengths, and values. When she shared her recipe with other leaders in the organization, it was an inspiration, and some of it became "best practice" for all leaders. And this sharing and inspiration also led to the development of a "leadership charter" for that organization.

To encourage knowledge sharing and learning, and catalyze development, we set up monthly global online meetings for all managers with the aim of presenting the results and trends around organizational happiness and share responses to these two things: (1) "What is working well?" and (2) "It would be even better if..."

Simple and powerful.

The Questions

Based on my work with the Happiness Sweet Spot, the science of happiness, and research on employment engagement, we have developed and carefully designed ten questions or statements that we know are related to organizational happiness and employee engagement. We are of course inspired by what other organizations and researchers have been developing in this area.[61]

Each of the questions is designed to be conducive to the three pillars of the Happiness Sweet Spot, organizational happiness, and employee engagement.

We can relate each of the questions to a research-based *why*, and each question is related to purpose, strengths, and compassion.

---

[61] Gallup's Q12 and some of the great work done by Nic Marks and his team at Happiness Work are good resources for inspiration in this area.

As a respondent you are asked to reflect about this week or period at work and respond to each statement by placing the marker on the scale somewhere between zero and 100. On average it takes ninety seconds to complete.

There is also an opportunity to give feedback and insight in a free text format by choosing the "What works well?" and/or "It would be even better if..." options after the questions.

For example, as I elaborated on in the chapter about strengths-based leadership,[62] the statement that according to research was found to have the biggest correlation to and effect on productivity was: "At work I have the opportunity to do what I do best every day."

That's why we use the statement "I have the opportunity to do what I do best" as number five. This is obviously related to the strengths pillar of the Happiness Sweet Spot.

---

62 According to Gallup research.

Also, with reference to Gallup, "Employees who have a manager who's always willing to listen to their work-related problems are 62 percent less likely to be burned out."

We use as number eight the statement, "I feel people care about me." This question is related to the compassion pillar of the Happiness Sweet Spot.

In this way each of the questions is tied to elements that are conducive to happiness as related to purpose, strengths, and compassion.

The 10 Questions in Your Motivational Landscape:

1. I feel happy at work.

PURPOSE

2. I'm proud of being part of my organization.
3. I know how I contribute to the mission of our organization.
4. I would recommend a friend for a job here.

STRENGTHS

5. I have the opportunity to do what I do best.
6. I have opportunities to learn, grow, and develop.
7. I have the resources available that enable me to do a good job.

COMPASSION

8. I feel people care about me.
9. I get recognition or praise (I am appreciated).
10. My opinion counts.

Every question is accompanied by an optional link where employees can elaborate by responding to these two prompts:

- What works well?
- It would be even better if...

The Motivational Landscape Data

I believe that data need to be simple and transparent so that we can decide how to act and be able to have meaningful conversations about strategy.

There are many employee engagement surveys on the market that are designed by human resources information technology service providers and use an algorithm that you need an expert to interpret. And still it can feel like a "black box" is between the respondent and the data we get. What's going on? Are the data reliable?

We don't think you need that. You already know why and how collecting and using that information helps your organization. As a leader you just need to have the raw data on a few relevant questions.

You need to see your Motivational Landscape based on transparent and reliable data so you can manage and lead your organization. I don't think you need an algorithm to do that.

The Motivational Landscape doesn't tell you what to do. You manage and lead your organization. Your Motivational Landscape tells you how it is.

And there is not a quick fix or a "one size fits all" solution that comes out of a black box or from interpreting an algorithm. Organizational happiness, leadership, and employee engagement cannot be facilitated effectively by spreadsheets or predetermined actions. That requires leadership and people decisions based on each unique organization and organism. You can't leave that to AI or machine learning.

First ask, "Where does it hurt?" Then take action.

You also want to know where it's awesome, so you can share and inspire best practice.

Some service providers in this area try to produce complex solutions, including a "if-this, then-that" kind of answer to your problem or pain. Although it can be tempting to outsource your tough decisions as a leader, it never works that way in reality. When you dare to lead, your organization will thrive.

An example[63] of how not to do it, I think, is the employee engagement pulse survey that refers you—with a telephone number—to a psychologist if an algorithm that measures input determines that your stress level is too high.

The challenges with stress and mental health in an organization cannot be outsourced like that. An app or a system cannot take away the responsibility to lead and manage. *We* need to lead and manage.

And we believe that our leaders can and will lead and manage.

---

[63] This is an example from a Danish governmental institution.

You and your leaders know your employees and organization, and we take it for granted that you can and will lead. That's your role. You can't outsource that or ask a system or a machine to do that.

The data in your Motivational Landscape are presented on a dashboard that gives you the Sweet Spot score and your scores for this period on purpose, strengths, and compassion on the organization as a whole and on each department in your organizational structure.

You can drill down through your Motivational Landscape data as much as you want, as long as the confidentiality is intact. That means a result is reported only if there are five or more respondents.

A well-known challenge with employee engagement surveys is the response rate. It's really a dilemma, because the higher the response rate, the better picture you get of your

Motivational Landscape and the more precise and accurate you can make your strategy and action plan.

There are many reasons for not responding. Employees may think it requires too much effort, or they may lack trust in the sense that they think it won't matter anyway, because nothing will change. Or they may not trust that the data won't somehow be traced to the individuals and that therefore they won't risk pointing out what's wrong or what really matters.

I think there is also a risk of *survey fatigue*. We are all asked to evaluate and respond every time we engage with an organization as a client or customer. "How was your experience today?" we hear, whether at the toilet, in the supermarket, after a visit to the dentist, or even after a phone call with a call center.

Therefore, it is important to show our employees that it matters—and that the time from input/response to reaction is short. We need to show that the Motivational Landscape data are being used and integrated.

Also at your Motivational Landscape, what you see as an employee immediately after you have responded to the last question is your own sweet spot score, and the score for your team and your organization so far that week.

LET'S GO TOGETHER

This book gives you a recipe for sustainable success, based on science, research, cases, our models, and tools.

Together with the Happiness Sweet Spot and Motivational Landscape this book is also a platform for inspiration and co-creation.

Use it and share it. We want to share our ideas, tell you what really works, and inspire you to start the organizational happiness journey for your team and your organization.

And we encourage you to share your story and insight with us. That way we—together—can catalyze and facilitate a movement that makes a difference by developing happy, sustainable, successful organizations and helps people and nations be happy.

Find our partners and me on our websites, and feel free to contact me and the team directly at info@TheHappinessSweetSpot.com.

www.TheHappinessSweetSpot.com

www.MotivationalLandscape.com

ACKNOWLEDGEMENTS

This book has been underway for some years. It has been a journey with many extraordinary and good people.

A big *thank-you!* to the organizations, leaders, and people with whom I have served and worked. Thank you for the inspiration and for your trust. This book is really about you—and for you.

Thank you to Ashley Hinson Dhakal for being an awesome designer, and thank you to Laurel Robinson for being so competent with the copyediting.

Thank you to Lotte, my soul mate and wife, for your unconditional love, support, and encouragement. You make me shine.

And to our four kids, Sofie, Tobias, Victor, and Albert, for keeping me on my toes, being an inspiration, and for believing in having dreams, the pursuit of happiness, and living with compassion. You are awesome!

BIBLIOGRAPHY

Aaker, Jennifer, Sara Gaviser Leslie, and Debra Schifrin. 2012. "The Business Case for Happiness. Stanford, CA: Stanford Graduate School of Business.

Achor, Shawn. 2011. "The Happiness Dividend." *Harvard Business Review*, June 23.

Autry, James. 2004. *The Servant Leader: How to Build a Creative Team, Develop Great Morale, and Improve Bottom-Line Performance*. New York: Three Rivers.

Barsade, Sigal, and Olivia A. O'Neill. 2014. "Employees Who Feel Love Perform Better," based on the research study "What's Love Got to Do with It? The Influence of a Culture of Companionate Love in the Long-Term Care Setting," in *Administrative Science Quarterly*. *Harvard Business Review*, January 13.

Bersin, Josh. 2015. "A New Market Is Born: Employee Engagement, Feedback, and Culture Apps." https://joshbersin.com/2015/09/a-new-market-is-born-employee-engagement-feedback-and-culture-apps/.

Brown, Brené. 2018. *Dare to Lead: Brave Work. Tough Conversations. Whole Hearts.* New York: Random House.

Brun, Pernille Hippe, David Cooperrider, and Mikke Ejsing. 2016. *Strengths-Based Leadership Handbook.* Brunswick, OH: Crown Custom Publishing.

Cooperrider, David, and Diana Whitney. 2005. *Appreciative Inquiry: A Positive Revolution in Change.* San Francisco: Berrett-Koehler.

Drucker, Peter F. 1967. *The Effective Executive*. New York: HarperCollins.

Duhigg, Charles. 2016. "What Google Learned From Its Quest to Build the Perfect Team." *New York Times Magazine*, February 25.

Fernández-Aráoz, Claudio. 2007. *Great People Decisions: Why They Matter So Much, Why They Are So Hard, and How You Can Master Them*. Hoboken, NJ: John Wiley.

Fernández-Aráoz, Claudio. 2013. "Learn How to Spot Portable Talent." *Harvard Business Review*, December.

George, Bill, Peter Sims, Andrew N. McLean, and Diana Mayer. 2007. "Discovering Your Authentic Leadership." *Harvard Business Review*, February.

Groysberg, Boris. 2010. *Chasing Stars: The Myth of Talent and the Portability of Performance*. Princeton, NJ: Princeton University Press.

Heidrick and Struggles. 2015. *The CEO Report: Embracing the Paradoxes of Leadership and the Power of Doubt.* https://www.heidrick.com/Knowledge-Center/Publication/The-CEO-Report.

Hsieh, Tony. 2010. *Delivering Happiness: A Path to Profits, Passion, and Purpose.* New York: Business Plus.

Marks, Nic. 2011. *The Happiness Manifesto.* New York: TED Books.

National Institute of Mental Health. "Prevalence of Any Mental Illness." Retrieved October 23, 2015, from http://www.nimh.nih.gov/health/statistics/prevalence/any-mental-illness-ami-among-adults.shtml.

Peterson, Christopher, and Martin Seligman. 2011. *Character Strengths and Virtues: A Handbook and Classification.* New York: Oxford University Press.

Rath, Tom. 2007. *StrengthsFinder 2.0.* New York: Gallup.

Rath, Tom, and Barry Conchie. 2009. *Strengths Based Leadership*. New York: Gallup.

Seligman, Martin E. P. 2011. *Flourish: A Visionary New Understanding of Happiness and Well-Being*. New York: Free Press.

Sinek, Simon. 2011. *Start with Why: How Great Leaders Inspire Everyone to Take Action*. New York: Penguin.

Sull, Donald N., and Kathleen M. Eisenhardt. 2015. *Simple Rules: How to Thrive in a Complex World*. London: John Murray.

Worline, Monica, and Jane Dutton. 2017. *Awakening Compassion at Work: The Quiet Power That Elevates People and Organizations*. Oakland, CA: Berrett-Koehler.

Zander, Rosamund Stone, and Benjamin Zander. 2002. *The Art of Possibility: Transforming Professional and Personal Life*. New York: Penguin.

20932074R00117

Printed in Great Britain
by Amazon